IMAGES
of America

LETCHWORTH STATE PARK

A visitor rests on one of the open gates of the Glen Iris Estate in 1875. Beyond him, the Portage iron bridge towers above the mists of the Upper Falls. The falls mark the beginning of the Genesee River's journey from the Portage gorge to the Mount Morris Highbanks. It is also here that the remarkable story of Letchworth State Park begins. (Author's collection.)

On the cover: Anna Letchworth (right) and classmates from Howland College of Union Springs pose on the rocks along the Lower Falls of the Genesee River in September 1874. Anna's uncle was William Pryor Letchworth, owner of the 1,000-acre Glen Iris Estate that he donated to New York State in 1907. Millions of visitors have since joined Anna and her classmates in experiencing the remarkable place called Letchworth State Park. (Author's collection.)

IMAGES
of America

LETCHWORTH STATE PARK

Thomas A. Breslin, Thomas S. Cook,
Russell A. Judkins, and Thomas C. Richens

ARCADIA
PUBLISHING

Published by Arcadia Publishing
Charleston, South Carolina

Library of Congress Catalog Card Number: 2007933650

For all general information contact Arcadia Publishing at:
Telephone 843-853-2070
Fax 843-853-0044
E-mail sales@arcadiapublishing.com
For customer service and orders:
Toll-Free 1-888-313-2665

Visit us on the Internet at www.arcadiapublishing.com

*This book is dedicated to William Pryor Letchworth and all those past
and present who have kept his spirit alive in Letchworth State Park.*

CONTENTS

ACKNOWLEDGMENTS

The authors wish to acknowledge the support and assistance of their wives, families, and friends in the completion of this volume. Anne Cook and Lucy Breslin, in particular, provided valuable counsel with editing and other matters. Likewise the authors wish to thank the Anthropology Department at the State University of New York at Geneseo, especially Beverly Rex-Burley and Ashley Treat.

Rebekah Collinsworth, editor at Arcadia Publishing, and Pam O'Neil, her predecessor, offered constant encouragement and prompt responses to the authors when they needed clarification of guidelines or other assistance. Their enthusiasm for the authors' vision of this book was the most important encouragement of all.

The following provided critical research support and several of the images for the work: Mary Jane York, Cathy Parker, and Jim and Linda Little of the Castile Historical Society; Amie Alden, Livingston County historian; Nunda Historical Society; Mary and Marri L. Ransom, Portage Town Historian's Office; Wyoming County Historian's Office; Warsaw Historical Society; Cayuga County historian; Museum of Art, Rhode Island School of Design; Kathryn Murano, Rochester Museum and Science Center; Frontenac Museum; Howland Stone Store Museum; Letchworth family; Don and Anne Reid; Randy, Barbara, and Sarah Richens; Patricia Wayne, Irondequoit town historian; U.S. Army Corps of Engineers, Mount Morris Dam; Robert E. Weir Jr; Cal DeGolyer; Dr. John Weaver; and Carson R. Waterman, artist, Seneca Nation of Indians, Snipe Clan.

Generous support and cooperation was offered by Letchworth State Park. It is reassuring that the historical and natural resources of Letchworth State Park are in such good hands. The authors sincerely thank Richard Parker, general park manager; Roland Beck, park manager; Brian Scriven, historic site manager; and Jeffrey W. Brooks, senior drafting technician. Leonora Brown, interpretive programs assistant, provided unremitting energy in pursuit of the research needs for this volume. Her extraordinary knowledge of the park and keen, well-trained eye, provided insights and background without which this book could not have been completed. To her, the authors collectively offer their sincere appreciation and admiration. Unless otherwise noted, photographs come from the authors' collections.

INTRODUCTION

Letchworth State Park is, by any measure, a special place. Stretching 17 miles along the Genesee River in western New York, the park boasts over 14,000 acres of natural beauty, including gorges, waterfalls, river flats, and forests. Recreational activities abound, and a variety of events and attractions bring hundreds of thousands of visitors throughout the year.

There is even more to the park, however, than the wonderful scenery and recreational opportunities. There is a story that is as old as the valley itself and as new as the last visitor to enter the park's gates. This story is the history of Letchworth State Park. Two main elements make up this remarkable story—the river and the people. These people decided, as William Pryor Letchworth once did, "that my lot should be cast here." Together these natural and human forces shaped the Genesee Valley and created the Letchworth State Park as it is known and loved today.

The story begins several thousand years ago at the end of the last Ice Age when an ancient Genesee River, responding to its new ice-free world, began to seek its original valley and primeval south-to-north passage once again. Its world had been entombed for ages by a grinding continental ice sheet a mile deep that had forever altered the original landscape, leaving behind deep, vast moraines of glacial tumuli and large, though temporary, glacial lakes. The Genesee River found itself diverted to a high plateau lateral to its original valley. But at Portage, the river began to cut a new passage north, beginning a journey that ended just beyond the Mount Morris Highbanks.

Humans first made their way to the Genesee River in this age of mastodons, giant cave bears, and condors. These paleo-people lived in small hunting bands, using the resources the changing landscape provided. They were the first of many generations of valley residents the Seneca people later called the "old ones." Archaeological evidence of these early native peoples has been found throughout the Genesee Valley and western New York.

By the 18th century, these lands were part of the territory of the Seneca, the "Keepers of the Western Door" of the great Iroquois league. The Ho-de-nau-sau-nee or "People of the Longhouse," as the Iroquois people called themselves, had planted the Great Tree of Peace generations before, and built villages from the Genesee River to the Hudson River and beyond. Three of those Seneca villages and countless seasonal camps existed in Sehgahunda (Seh-ga-hunda), the name they gave to the place that is now Letchworth State Park. The Seneca knew the valley and environs as a special place the Creator had provided for them and the many generations that were to follow.

One Seneca who lived along the Genesee River was Deh-ge-wa-nus, also known as Mary Jemison, the "White Woman of the Genesee." Captured on the frontier of Pennsylvania during the French and Indian War and adopted by the Seneca, Mary Jemison came to the Gardeau Flats in present-day Letchworth State Park in 1779. Her Seneca name meant "two falling voices" and describes well the remarkable woman who was important in both the native and white worlds. When America's western frontier reached the Genesee Valley, the Seneca sold most of the valley, reserving two tracts of land within the present park boundaries as reservations. The Gardeau reservation was set aside for Mary Jemison and her extended family.

Mary Jemison lived at Gardeau for over 50 years, becoming a woman highly respected by both the Seneca and the pioneers who settled near her. The Jemison family was the last of the Seneca to leave their homes in Sehgahunda, moving to the Buffalo Creek reservation in 1831. Although the Seneca people no longer live along the Genesee Valley in Letchworth State Park, their presence has never disappeared. To this day, their story, images, place names, cultural elements, and descendants remain an important part of Letchworth State Park.

The pioneers were the next group to shape the landscape. The men and women who settled this frontier brought their own names for the land and their own ways of life. Sehgahunda became Portage, named for the great carrying trail around the falls and gorge. For two generations, the settlers worked to build their homes, farms, and businesses in these rugged lands. They built mills to harness the river, cut the ancient forests to feed the mills and clear their fields, and established several communities that one day became the "vanished villages" of Letchworth State Park. Today many of these settlers rest in the Pioneer Cemetery in the park.

Two great engineering projects marked the end of the settlement period of the Portage Falls. They were the Genesee Valley canal and the Portage wooden bridge. Together they altered the history and landscape of the future park lands.

The Genesee Valley canal did what the Genesee River could not do—it carried boats heavy with freight and passengers from the Erie Canal to the Allegheny River. The workers who dug the canal knew the area along the Portage gorge as the "nine mile nightmare." The images from that era show why.

Equally amazing was the Portage wooden bridge, constructed across the gorge above the Upper Falls. This train trestle became a popular stop for passengers riding the Erie Railroad and for the photographers who took wonderful views of the "Highest Wooden Bridge in the World" to peddle to tourists as they stood on the dizzying heights. Although a disaster destroyed the wooden bridge, a new iron trestle, almost as impressive, replaced it in record time. That bridge is the one that still stands. Both of these railroad trestles shaped the landscape and played important parts in the park's history.

The Portage wooden bridge is credited with bringing William Pryor Letchworth into the story. "Mister Letchworth," as he is still called by many area residents and park employees, was only 35 years old when his train stopped on the Portage bridge in 1858. Within a year, he paid a little more than $37 per acre for nearly 200 acres of the valley near the Upper and Middle Falls. Over the next 50 years, he created the 1,000-acre Glen Iris Estate, named for the rainbows often seen at the Middle Falls.

Letchworth is one of the most remarkable men of the 19th century. Born to a Quaker family in northeastern New York State, he became a successful industrialist through hard work and innovation, both in new production methods and progressive labor relations. He was, however, much more than a successful businessman. He left his mark on the world in several more important ways.

First and foremost was his Glen Iris Estate that reflected his real passions in life, including art, literature, history, and conservation. Although he never married or raised a family, his house and grounds were usually filled with the laughter and fellowship of his relatives and friends who saw the Glen Iris Estate as a great adventure and a respite from the worries of the world. The estate's gates were open to the public, and thousands came to enjoy the restored beauty of the Middle Falls, the awesome power of the Genesee River as it tumbled through the flume at Lower Falls, or to wander along the many scenic trails carefully laid out along the beautiful gorge.

Letchworth made sure all visitors left both inspired and enlightened. On the bluff above the Glen Iris, he built an early museum complex to help preserve and present the history of the Genesee Valley. He brought the Seneca Council House from Caneadea to the Council Grounds and held ceremonies known as the "Last Council Fire." When Mary Jemison's grave in the old Buffalo Creek burial grounds was threatened by the urban expansion of Buffalo, Letchworth reburied her near the Council House. In his last public appearance before his death in 1910, he dedicated the statue that still stands over the grave of this remarkable woman. Letchworth also edited several editions of her life story that she had dictated to a local doctor in 1823.

The Seneca adopted Letchworth in 1872 in recognition of his work on the Council Grounds. The name he was given, Hai-wa-ye-is-tah, means "the man who always does right."

The title was more than fitting. Although most remember him for the park that bears his name, Letchworth spent over 30 years giving his time, talents, and money to help the disadvantaged in New York and America. After his retirement at the age of 48, he became a member of the New York State Board of Charities, the forerunner of today's social service agencies. For over 30 years, he worked to improve prison conditions, helped orphans and poor children, developed the foster care system and industrial school system, and promoted the development of institutions to help epileptics and the mentally ill. He traveled the world researching the latest methods and programs and wrote or edited over 70 books and pamphlets, including the influential *Care and Treatment of Epileptics*, published in 1900.

Letchworth's original plan was to have his estate become a refuge for orphan children operated by the Wyoming Benevolent Association. But when powerful interests announced plans for a dam just above the Portage Falls, Letchworth decided to offer the 1,000-acre estate to the State of New York. Gov. Charles E. Hughes signed the bill, creating Letchworth State Park in January 1907.

Letchworth died on December 1, 1910, and was buried at Forest Lawn Cemetery in Buffalo. The challenge from that point on was to create a modern public park from a private estate while maintaining Letchworth's vision and mission that was, as he wrote in 1907, to "preserve for the enjoyment and elevation of mankind those places in our land possessing rare natural beauty, the charms of which, once destroyed, can never be restored."

The development of the new park began under the American Scenic and Historic Preservation Society. Andrew H. Green founded the society in 1895 to "acquire and hold for public enjoyment historic places and objects and areas of picturesque natural scenery." The society was already managing several state reservations, including those at Niagara Falls, Stony Point Battlefield, Watkins Glen, and now, Letchworth State Park. The society's Letchworth State Park Committee, which included Letchworth's personal secretary Caroline Bishop as librarian and museum curator, oversaw the transformation of the park until 1930, when the Genesee State Park Commission was formed.

The expansion and development of the 20th-century park was the direct result of the cultural, political, and economic changes that swept the country. The automobile became the driving force behind a new type of tourist who wanted more facilities, new kinds of recreational opportunities, and easier access to scenic and historic sites in the park. The Great Depression, World War II, and postwar changes all impacted Letchworth State Park. By the 1960s, despite the changes and challenges, Letchworth State Park reached the Mount Morris Highbanks where recreational facilities were built to accommodate the modern park visitor. Beyond the Mount Morris Highbanks, with its mighty Mount Morris dam, the waters of the Genesee River return once more to the river's preglacial valley.

The story of Letchworth State Park is woven by the power of nature and the constant renewal of the cycle of life along the Genesee River. Whether portaging their canoes, establishing villages, or building a modern park, humans have followed the course of an ancient river and built on dreams of their predecessors. The result is a special place that is both a commemoration to those who have come before and a testament to the great enduring gifts of nature and earth, which although ever changing, forever continue.

The purpose of this book is to present the story of Letchworth State Park through images and artifacts taken from the park's remarkable history. Whether the work is enjoyed at home or used as a historical guidebook on a visit to the park, it is hoped that it will help the reader understand why Letchworth State Park is a special place, a heritage to be shared and enjoyed by all.

September 2007

One

THE FALLS

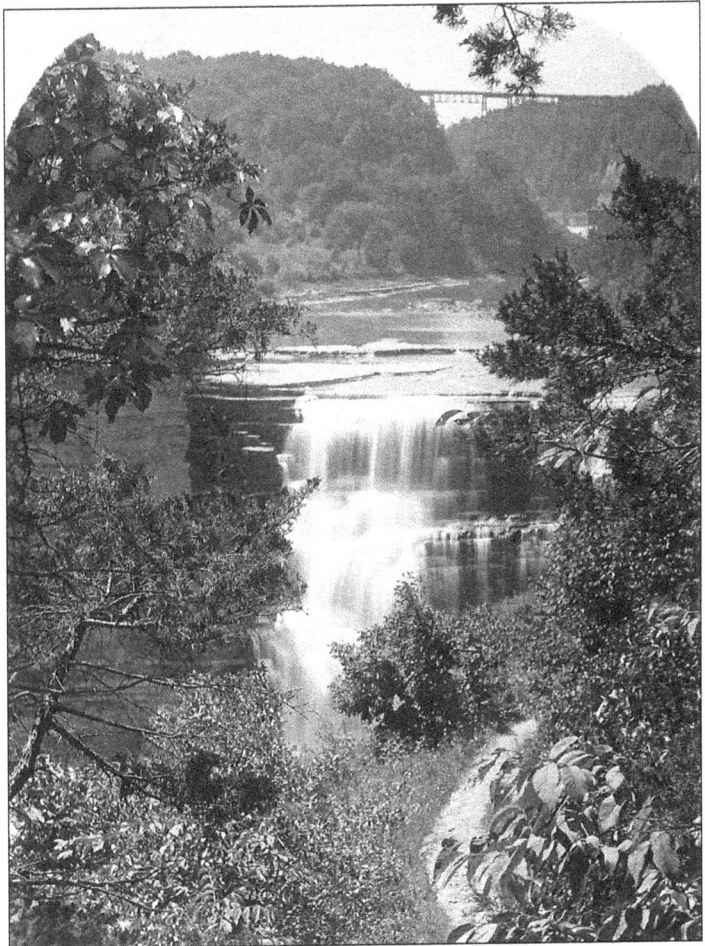

The waters of the Genesee River tumble over the Middle Falls in this stereo postcard that was taken a few years after the creation of Letchworth State Park. An old trail, worn by many generations of inhabitants and visitors, leads beyond the Middle Falls to the Upper Falls and Portage High Bridge in the distance. All are reminders of the natural and human forces that have shaped these lands and have written the history of Letchworth State Park. It is fitting that here, at the Portage Falls of the Genesee River, the story begins.

When the Genesee River reaches Portageville, it is forced to the west by a ridge of glacial till left by retreating ice sheets millennia ago. This 1890s image, looking east toward that bend, also shows the beginning of the centuries-old carrying road used to portage around the Portage Falls. Although this stagecoach road is now closed, hikers can still follow the trail through Letchworth State Park.

This photograph, probably taken in the 1920s, shows the Genesee River entering the Portage gorge at what was called the "Rock Cut" in canal and railroad days. This marks the beginning of a 17-mile journey that ends at the Mount Morris Highbanks. This image was taken just north of the modern Portageville entrance to the park. (Letchworth State Park.)

12

According to Arthur C. Parker's *Skunny Wundy and Other Indian Tales*, "When our green earth was young and Ra-wen-io roamed about making all things pleasant for mankind's appearance, there was one spot where all the Ancient Ones loved to come for a rest. It was a place called Seh-ga-hun-da, the Vale of Three Falls." With the Upper Falls in the distance, this 1880s view hints at what Segahunda was like when the village of Deowesta (De-o-wes-ta) stood on the hilltop seen left of the falls. This was also the place where Mona-sha-sha and her young son were swept over the Middle Falls long ago, their spirits returning in the form of white deer sometimes seen in the park. The power of the river can be seen in the postcard below that shows the Upper and Middle Falls in March 1916.

From the story-telling traditions of the Seneca, one learns from Arthur C. Parker's *Skunny Wundy and Other Indian Tales*, "When Ra-wen-io had finished his tasks and created the tribes of men, he made caves in the cliffs of the Gen-ne-see and divided the Jungies into three tribes that they might bring peace and plenty to the pleasant river." (Original illustration, copyright 2007 by Carson R. Waterman.)

Also quoted from Parker, "Oh you who are Stone Throwers . . . you shall dwell in the caves at the fall called Het-ge-oh the first one. Here you shall make stone hammers for all the tribes of men who are to come." This is Hetgeoh, the 70-foot-high Upper Falls from the eastern bank in 1892. Some 19th-century photographers called this Horseshoe Falls.

14

According to Parker, "Oh, you who are the Under Water Jungies . . . your home shall be in the caves and crannies at Ska-ga-dee the Middle Falls, and in the pools below the falling waters you shall guard all the springs that give forth sweet water to quench the thirst of men and their brother fur-folk." This unusual view was taken from a small cave visible near the 107-foot falls.

Below the Middle Falls, the waters have cut towering cliffs over 200 feet high. These visitors have climbed down the wooden stairs that once existed along Dehgayasoh (Deh-ga-ya-soh) Creek to reach the riverbed. The beautiful cascade they seem to be enjoying was known as Bridal Veil Falls and no longer exists. It was actually a waste weir for the canal that ran at the top of the cliff.

The Big Tree Treaty of 1797 opened the Genesee Valley for settlement. By 1820, pioneers had arrived in the falls area. Reuben and Perry Jones were first, followed by many others. Among them was Urania Fancher, shown here. She came to the falls in her 30s and lived almost 50 years along the Portage gorge. The Fancher's loom stood for years in the Nancy Jemison cabin on the Council Grounds. (Fancher/Davis/Beyer Family.)

The artist Thomas Cole sketched Dehgayasoh Creek during a visit to the falls in 1839. Shown here is his 1847 painting made from that sketch, titled *Genesee Scenery*. The image shows some of the early development including a bridge, the nearby Davis house, and a cabin near the present-day Council Grounds. (Museum of Art, Rhode Island School of Design, Jesse Metcalf Fund.)

16

When these pioneers came, Skagadee was still a thing of beauty, surrounded by great forests. Settlers at the falls needed to make a living. The Middle Falls was a source of power, running mills that turned the forests into lumber demanded by towns and cities. Alvah Palmer built a log cabin and a sawmill near the falls by 1824. Three decades later, a complex of mills clung to the riverbank and, as the 1850s stereo view at right shows, stacks of lumber were all that was left of the trees that once covered the hillside. A fire in January 1859 destroyed the main mills, but the milldam, lattice bridge, and a smaller mill still stood in the early 1860s as shown below. The lattice bridge was destroyed in the flood of 1865.

No. 125.—VIEW ON THE GENESEE RIVER, PORTAGE, NEAR NEW YORK

Some local residents dreamed of creating a prospering mill town at the Middle Falls. The name of Portage Falls Village was even proposed and a map drawn. This structure, shown near the falls in the 1860s, was said to have been a store. But lack of cheap and reliable transportation dashed the dream, even though a canal and railroad were soon built nearby.

Although the canal was started first, the railroad was the first modern means of transportation to reach Portage Falls. Called the "crystal palace of all bridges" when completed in 1852, it was said to be the highest and longest bridge in the world. Folklore has a 14-year-old designing the structure, but Buffalo and New York City railroad chief engineer Silas Seymour was the real designer and builder.

18

1852.

CELEBRATION

OF THE

COMPLETION OF THE HIGH BRIDGE

ACROSS GENESEE RIVER AT PORTAGE,

ON THE

BUFFALO AND NEW-YORK CITY RAIL ROAD,

ON WEDNESDAY, AUGUST 25, 1852.

DINNER BILL OF FARE.

SOUP

Bean,   St. Julienne.

FISH.

Boiled Salmon, Parsley sauce,   Lobsters.
Boiled striped Bass, Oyster Sauce,   Brook Trout, Fried,
Mackinaw Trout boiled   Chowder.

BOILED.

Mutton, Caper sauce,   Tongue,
Boiled Turkey, Oyster sauce,   Corned Beef,
Boiled Chicken, Egg sauce,   Ham,

ROAST.

Beef, from an Ox presented by George B. Chase,
WEIGHT 2,800 LBS.

The story of the Portage wooden bridge begins and ends in tragedy. A grand celebration was held on the flats between Upper and Middle Falls on August 25, 1852. Ten thousand people flocked to see Gov. Washington Hunt christen the magnificent structure and to partake in the great barbecue. The silk menu from that day, shown in part, included a large ox donated by George B. Chase. It is thought that the roasted ox was tainted, because many fell ill after the ceremonies. Two dozen died, including Eben Warner, a doctor from nearby Nunda. (Castile Historical Society.)

Later part of the Erie Railroad, the Portage High Bridge became a popular tourist attraction. Handbills passed out on passenger trains proclaimed it to be one of the "Grandest Views on the Western Continent" and announced it to be "800 feet long, and 235 feet high, containing over 1,600,000 feet of timber and 108,862 pounds of iron. It took all of the available timber on 205 acres of heavy timbered land." Trains, such as the one in the stereo view image at left, stopped at the Portage station and gave passengers a chance to walk out on the bridge. Adventurous souls could climb down stairs to catwalks through the lower levels of the bridge. The image below, probably taken around 1870, is titled *Among the Timbers* and shows a group enjoying the view.

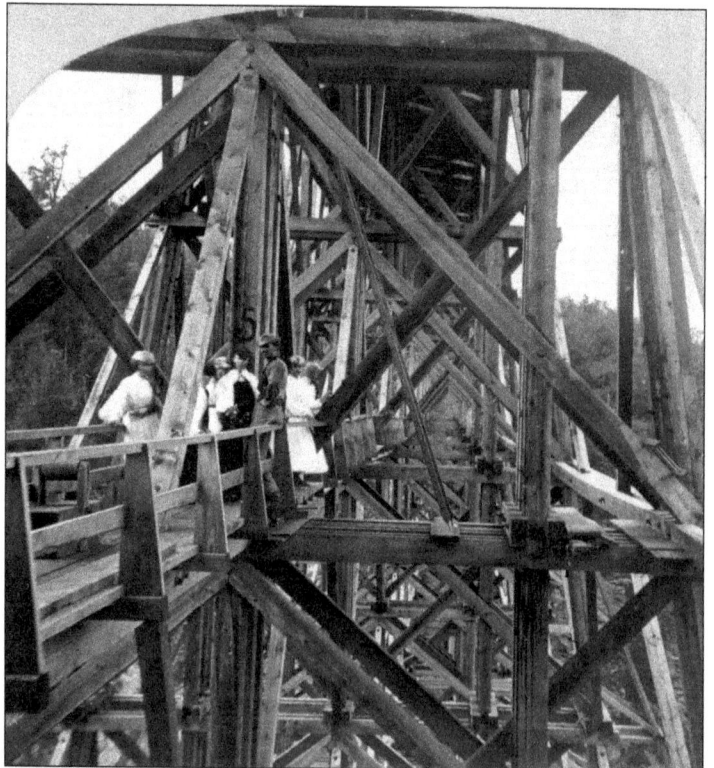

The greatest threat to the bridge was fire. Water barrels were placed at both ends of the trestle and watchmen were required to walk the length of the bridge after the passing of a train because of the danger of sparks. Sightseers were also cautioned. One of the boys in this image is standing next to a sign warning that, "Smoking strictly forbidden on or about this bridge."

802. AMONG THE TIMBERS OF BRIDGE, PORTAGE, N. Y.

Disaster struck on May 6, 1875. A watchman discovered a fire around 1:00 a.m., but was unable to stop the spreading flames. William Pryor Letchworth watched from the Glen Iris and wrote, "The spectacle presented at precisely four o'clock was fearfully grand, every timber in the bridge seemed then to be ignited, and an open network of the fire was stretched across the upper end of the valley."

21

In the days after the fire, local folks and photographers flocked to see the ruins of the bridge. All that remained were charred timbers and the stone pillars that once held the magnificent structure. Among those who documented the disaster were photographers George Washburn of Castile (above) and L. E. Walker of Warsaw (left). Since the line was a critical link between Buffalo and New York City, the contract for the construction of a new bridge was signed with the Watson Manufacturing Company only four days after the fire. This may have led to the persistent rumor that the Erie Railroad company started the blaze to raze the old wooden structure so a new iron trestle could be built.

George Morison, an engineer for the Erie Railroad, was given the task of designing and building the new bridge. Even though the first load of iron girders was delayed, the first tower was completed by June 13, 1875. This photograph, probably taken by Washburn in late June or early July, shows the steady progress made by Morison and his crew. The work was completed in an astonishing 84 days. (Mary Jane York.)

Portage Bridge half action

The new Portage bridge was finished on July 29, 1875. Two days later, L. E. Walker captured this historic moment, when the six-engine test-train stopped on the bridge, their crews standing on their engines to wave to the crowds of onlookers. This new structure was 20 feet higher than the old bridge and consisted of 1.3 million pounds of iron. The cost was $80,000, less than half the cost of the original wooden trestle.

23

Since 1875, the Portage High Bridge has played an important role in the American transportation system. During World War I, soldiers, living in a small encampment near the west end of the bridge, guarded the trestle from possible saboteurs. It continues to carry many freight trains across the gorge. This image is titled *Side view of the New Iron Bridge, Portage, N.Y.*

Although the modern bridge still has 1875 on the base of one of its great towers, it has undergone several renovations. During work in 1903, for example, about 260 tons of iron were replaced with new steel. This photograph shows workers reinforcing the bridge during World War II. (Castile Historical Society.)

In this stereo view, taken between 1875 and 1878, the Portage bridge towers above the Genesee River. To the right of the river is another ribbon of water, the Genesee Valley Canal. It was, for a short time, possible to get on a canal boat at the Upper Falls and travel all the way to New York City or head south as far as the Gulf of Mexico.

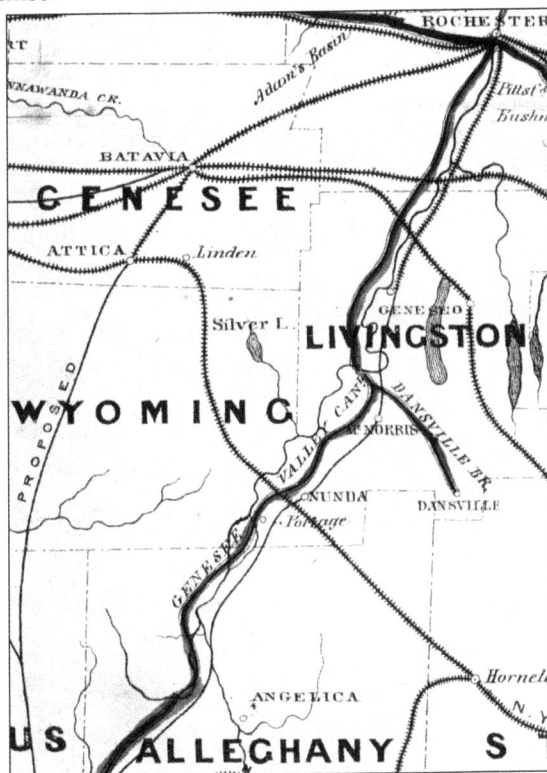

This map appeared in an 1859 report by the state engineer and surveyor. The Genesee Valley Canal began at the Erie Canal in Rochester and followed the Genesee River south through Portage, eventually linking with the Allegheny-Ohio-Mississippi River system. Where canal and railroad cross to form an X just below the center of the map is the exact spot shown in the photograph above.

Work on the canal began in 1836 and reached Mount Morris in 1840. Beyond Nunda, 17 locks were built to lift the canal to the hilltop near the Portage gorge. There work began on a tunnel through the cliff that would be 1,082 feet long, 27 feet high, and 20 feet wide. This 1843 engraving looks downstream from the Upper Falls. In the center, the Genesee River drops over the Middle Falls. To the right, high on the cliff, is Hornby Lodge, home of contractor Elisha Johnson. Below Johnson's home, the southern entrance of the tunnel can be seen. Little remains of Hornby Lodge save a rustic couch exhibited in the park's museum and a door. The sketch of Hornby Lodge, seen below, appeared in *Historical Collection of the State of New York* by John Barber and Henry Howe in 1844.

Hornby Lodge at Portage Falls.

A financial panic and loose rock spelled the end of the tunnel. Engineers instead blasted a man-made shelf for the canal 200 feet above the Genesee River. This image, taken from Inspiration Point, shows the canal and towpath on top of the cliff on the left. Beyond a small shed beside the canal is a wooden aqueduct that carried the canal over an area known for landslides to this day.

The canal was 42 feet wide at the surface, 26 feet wide at the bottom, and four feet deep. From the slide area, it followed the bank under the Portage bridge and then through the Rock Cut. At this point, the towpath was also a public highway, which ran to the lattice bridge across the Middle Falls. These two images come from the 1865 to 1875 period.

Frozen Aquaduct, Portage, N. Y.

At Portageville, the canal crossed the Genesee River on the Portageville aqueduct. Built on stone abutments 40 feet high, the structure cost $70,000 to build and more to maintain. Although most of the water was drained from the canal during the winter months, enough remained to create this frozen scene captured by L. E. Walker around 1870. The wing wall seen at the far end of the aqueduct still stands today.

The entire canal was completed in 1862 at a cost of nearly $7 million. The man-made waterway was almost 125 miles long, had 112 locks, more than a dozen aqueducts, and over 200 bridges. For 16 years, thousands of canal boats, like the one shown here loading bluestone from a quarry south of Portageville, plied the waters above the gorge, carrying tons of freight and hundreds of passengers.

Maintenance costs and competition from the expanding railroad network hurt the canal. The state closed it after the 1878 season and sold the right-of-way. The Genesee Valley Canal Railroad was built in 1882 and later became part of the Pennsylvania Railroad. This postcard from the early 1900s shows a train heading north on tracks laid over the old canal. The "Pennsy" operated until the early 1960s.

The canal was still operating when this view was made from the Portage bridge in the late 1860s. The canal, drained for the winter, is on the lower right. Across the hillside are the homes of families that, like the Seneca before them, enjoyed life in the beautiful lands of Sehgahunda. Among them was William Pryor Letchworth, who first saw this view of the Portage Falls in 1858.

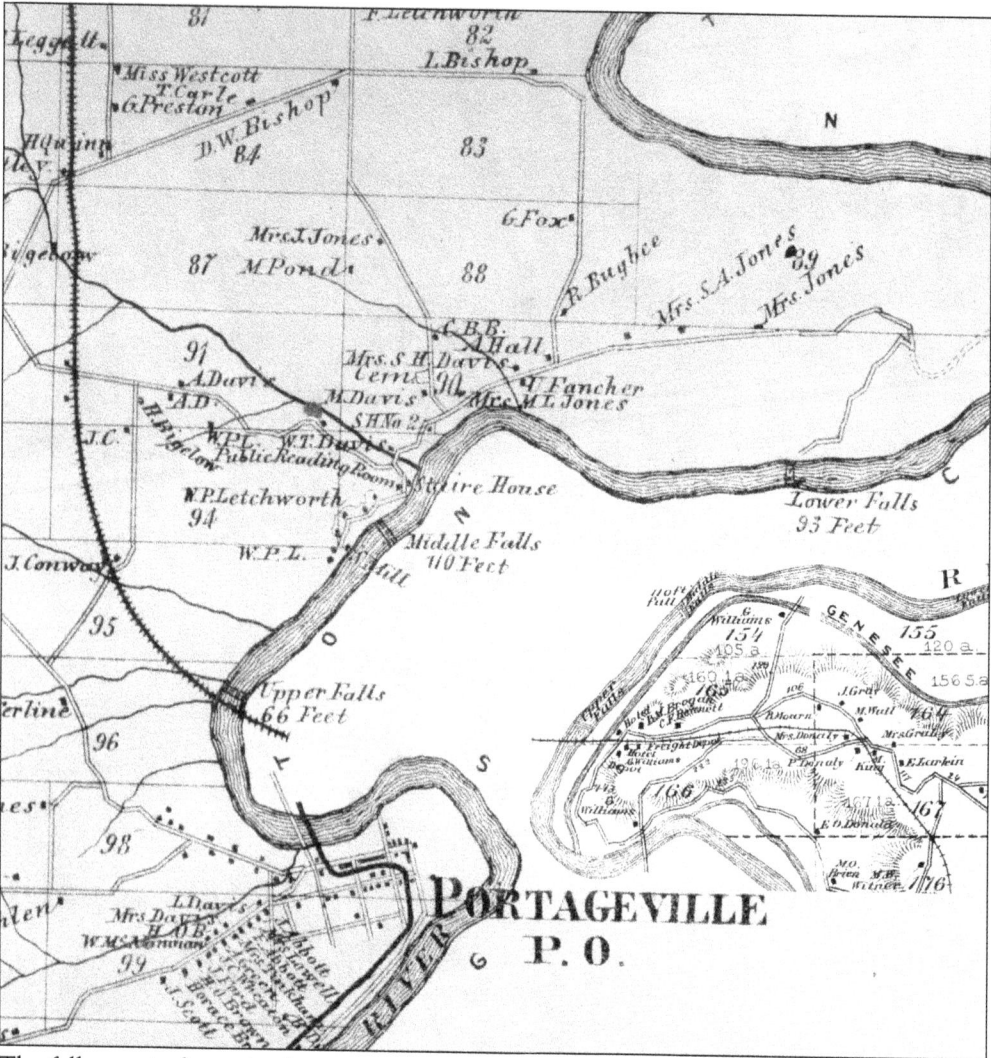

The falls area is shown in this composite image of the 1866 town of Genesee Falls (Wyoming County) and (the inset) 1872 town of Portage (Livingston County) maps. Much had changed since the days of the Seneca village of Deowesta, which once flourished on the hilltop east of the Upper Falls. The old trails and portages had given way to roads, the canal, and the railroad, connecting farms and businesses along the Genesee River with their neighbors and far-away markets. Also shown on the map is property that became Letchworth State Park a half century later.

Two

GLEN IRIS

William Pryor Letchworth was highly successful in business by the age of 33 when this picture was taken. Born into a Quaker family in Brownville on May 26, 1823, Letchworth built a fortune with his company Pratt and Letchworth. When he first set eyes upon the Portage Falls in 1858 during a railway journey, he clearly had a strong reaction to the stunning landscape. Letchworth's initial purchase was 190 acres in 1859 from Michael Smith. He did not seek to develop the area for financial gain, but rather his aim was to enjoy the natural landscape and build his estate. Renewal and improvement became recurring themes over the next 50 years Letchworth was to spend at his beloved Glen Iris Estate. (Letchworth State Park.)

By the age of 25, Letchworth partnered with Pascal Pratt to create Pratt and Letchworth. The Buffalo business held patents to manufacture malleable iron, produced saddlery and Japanware, and made toys. The factories above are part of the Pratt and Letchworth works near Buffalo. (Letchworth State Park.)

Milling operations devastated the old growth forests in the area, which were nearly stripped bare when Letchworth first arrived. Letchworth saw a countryside desperately in need of rejuvenation and had the foresight to restore and protect this extraordinary spot in western New York. (Letchworth State Park.)

Letchworth Park in Danger

A Plea for Its Defence
by the

American Scenic and Historic Preservation Society

Headquarters: Tribune Building, New York City

Many have tried to harness the power of the Genesee River in this gorge. On April 29, 1898, the Genesee River Company was established to build a dam near Portage. Letchworth opposed this plan and turned to the American Scenic and Historic Preservation Society, founded in 1895 by Andrew H. Green to help establish and protect areas like Central Park in New York City. After failing to raise the necessary funds, the Genesee River Company's five-year charter came to an end in 1903. The company reappeared in 1906, but Letchworth thwarted their efforts again by donating his estate to the State of New York. If Letchworth had not arrived when he did, the area would undoubtedly be very different today. (Letchworth State Park.)

William Pryor Letchworth spent 50 years building, protecting, and enjoying his cherished Glen Iris Estate and in the 1860s called upon the talents of William Webster, an apprentice of Frederick Law Olmstead, to beautify the grounds. Taken from the Council Grounds, this perspective is fascinating because the wooden bridge in the distance was where Letchworth first saw this area. Part of Webster's design is the pond and fountain, which still exists today.

The Glen Iris of today is the result of numerous architectural changes. The left portion started as a cabin built by Alvah Palmer in the 1820s. The right, main section was added by Michael Smith in the 1830s and used as a temperance tavern. Letchworth insisted on preserving the structure as the Glen Iris Estate grew. This view was taken before a third floor was added in 1880.

Although Letchworth never married, he was the fourth of eight children and frequently entertained his family at his estate. This unique portrait shows members of the Letchworth family relaxing on the porch of the Glen Iris. From left to right are Letchworth, steadying the chair of his grandniece Mary Darling; his sister, Mary Ann Crozer (seated); their cousin, Ann Eliza "Cousin Lill" McCloud; and a family group including William Darling with his wife, Adella, another one of Letchworth's nieces. (Letchworth State Park.)

This rare interior photograph of the Glen Iris taken by McCloud reflects Letchworth's tastes. The portrait of Letchworth's mother, Anne Hance Letchworth, hangs on the far wall of the parlor to this very day. (Letchworth State Park.)

Letchworth shared the beauty of his estate with the public and allowed visitors on the grounds with few restrictions. Some even peered through his windows while he dined. This group (also shown on the cover) includes his niece Anna Letchworth and is chaperoned by Charlotte Letchworth, wife of Letchworth's brother George. Anna and her classmates left her uncle a poem that included the following lines: "We'll look to Glen Iris in grateful affection, And live our bright Portage days over again."

William Pryor Letchworth revitalized the forest by planting thousands of trees while also sculpting and decorating the area. This fountain at Glen Iris Estate, new roads, gardens, and "crystal lakes" were part of William Webster's original rustic design. (Letchworth State Park.)

This group posed for their photograph on the south lawn of the Glen Iris Estate on a warm, summer day. Their train crossed the wooden Portage bridge in the background.

This group of tourists is enjoying a picnic off the beaten path overlooking the Portage gorge. Perhaps this was a favorite shady spot where they could enjoy the tranquility of the grounds, the fresh air, and rich aroma of pine.

Pennsylvania
RAILROAD
BUFFALO AND ALLEGHENY VALLEY DIVISION.

A BASKET PICNIC—TAKE YOUR FAMILY!

LABOR-DAY EXCURSION
TO
PORTAGE FALLS,

Monday, SEPTEMBER 3, 1900.

FILL your lunch basket, take your family and friends and spend a delightful day at . . .

Portage Falls

and the surrounding country, unsurpassed for beauty and grandeur. The three Falls, together with the picturesque walks, groves and ravines, make it a veritable fairyland. Historical GLEN IRIS, the estate of W. P. Letchworth, with its beautiful lawns and walks, is always a place of interest to the traveler. Here may be seen the old Indian Council House and many Indian curiosities. Near by is the grave of Mary Jamison, known as the "White Woman of the Genesee."

Excellent Hotels.

Through the Beautiful Genesee Valley.

Returning at an Early Hour.

Children between the age of 5 and 12 years half fare.

Railway excursions "through the beautiful Genesee Valley" gave tourists the opportunity to experience the magnificent views of Portage Falls and the "Historical Glen Iris, with its beautiful lawns and walks." Although William Pryor Letchworth opened his estate to the public, the overwhelming number of visitors eventually became a concern. At one point, he even attempted to stop Sunday train excursions. Access and overuse are still issues today.

After traveling in Europe, Letchworth became fond of Swiss architecture and built several Swiss-style cottages on his grounds. Lauterbrunnen, pictured here in 1915, was built to accommodate his family and guests. After Letchworth donated his estate to the State of New York, the cottage was used as housing for park superintendents.

George Williams built the Cascade House in 1853 near the Portage bridge and the hotel provided lodging to many upper-class railway tourists. One visitor, in a letter to the *Nunda News* in 1876, described the hotel as having "grand and commodious accommodations for the rich and aristocratic." The hotel burned in 1969. (Castile Historical Society.)

Eagle Hill, once decorated with the eagle statue above, marked the path leading to Lauterbrunnen. Although the eagle is gone, the name remains. Letchworth named many of the special places within his estate, and through these names, his legacy and vision continues. (Letchworth State Park.)

William Pryor Letchworth had stone walls built along the roads of his Glen Iris Estate. Some of these original walls still exist today, making a ride through Letchworth State Park seem like a journey through history. (Letchworth State Park.)

L. E. Walker, Publisher, Warsaw, N. Y.

Gems from American Scenery.

Numerous photographers captured the Glen Iris Estate on hundreds of stereo views sold to tourists. A stereo view, two photographs mounted side by side, provides a three-dimensional image when placed in a special viewer. This one captures the tranquility of Glen Iris where Letchworth could escape the demands of business. Beyond the pond is the ivy-covered Glen Iris. The canoe, christened Monashasha after the white deer legend, floats in the "crystal lake."

Letchworth's formal gardens were located on the site of the present-day museum. These unidentified men trimming the gardens' hedge were among dozens of local people who worked for Letchworth, including his personal secretary, Caroline Bishop, and several members of her family. Glen Iris Estate was Letchworth's personal canvas, but it required the hard work of many people to maintain.

William Pryor Letchworth cared about the local community and his neighbors and made numerous improvements to the surrounding area. He personally paid for this decorative cast-iron bridge over Dehgayasoh Creek near the road to the Council Grounds. In the background is Mariah Davis's home and refreshment stand that sold homemade root beer for 5¢ a glass.

These men in 19th-century dress are stopping for a rest along a trail still in use today that runs between Glen Iris Estate and Middle Falls. This rustic shelter was known as the Mineral Spring to early visitors and a spot where one could get a cold drink of water on a hot and humid western New York day. One story says the Mineral Springs was actually the overflow from the fountain and pond.

This wooden overlook provided a spectacular view of the Middle Falls and is an example of the numerous improvements made to assure scenic access and safety for visitors.

MIDDLE FALL OF GENESEE RIVER AT PORTAGE, N. Y.

These two women are enjoying the natural setting on a bridge over Degewanus (De-ge-wa-nus) Creek near the Upper Falls. A group of Letchworth's friends and relatives, referring to themselves as the "Nameless Club," named quite a few landmarks on his estate. Letchworth and the club members named the creek Degewanus (or Dehgewanus), which was Mary Jemison's Seneca name.

43

William Pryor Letchworth owned several farms on his estate where he bred and raised registered shorthorn cattle in the 1880s. Letchworth acquired the cattle on a trip to the Bluegrass region of Kentucky and in a letter home wrote, "We shall have the satisfaction of feeling that we have done something that may improve the herds of western New York." Some of the Swiss cowbells hang in the stairway of the Glen Iris Inn today.

After his retirement in the early 1870s, Letchworth accepted an appointment to the New York State Board of Charities. Ever the champion of children's causes, he opened his Prospect Home farm to orphans from Buffalo so they could enjoy the fresh air. The children came in groups of 10 and stayed for three days, one of which was spent at Glen Iris Estate. Prospect Home is now part of the park administration center. The carriage was purchased by Letchworth to take visitors around the estate.

This photograph of the Middle Falls, taken from the Pennsylvania Railroad, shows a rejuvenated landscape, drastically different than Letchworth's first view in 1858. It took 50 years to accomplish these changes, and to ensure their preservation, he offered his Glen Iris Estate to the State of New York. The gift was accepted in January 1907 and Letchworth State Park was officially established.

After William Pryor Letchworth's death in 1910, his charitable acts and kind character were noted by the Honorable Truman L. Stone in a tribute titled *Reminiscences of William P. Letchworth*. "I had the privilege of a personal and somewhat intimate acquaintance with Mr. Letchworth for nearly thirty years and that during the period of his life when the brightest qualities of mind in him were at the best. During that time I learned to know of his uprightness of character and purity of friendship. He had a heart as intensely kind and as nobly true as ever God gave to one of his creatures. I never heard him say one deprecating word of any man or men's work; I never knew him to let pass without some remonstrance, or endeavor to mitigate, a blameful word spoken of another. His greatest characteristic was firmness of mind and body which rendered him capable of the most delicate sensations and sympathies." Letchworth indeed lived up to the name given to him by the Iroquois Confederacy, Hai-wa-ye-is-tah, meaning "the Man Who Always Does Right." (Letchworth State Park.)

46

Three

COUNCIL GROUNDS

The Council Grounds on a bluff above the Glen Iris were entered through a shaded maple grove that was planted by William Pryor Letchworth. A now-vanished section of the legendary Big Tree, the most famous of the Genesee Valley oaks, was sheltered at lane's end. The Seneca-Iroquois Council House from Caneadea, which Letchworth rescued from destruction, is next to the Big Tree enclosure. The peaceful grave and final resting place of Mary Jemison, the captive "White Woman of the Genesee," marked by its monument, is also on the left, overlooking her beloved Genesee River. Her daughter Nancy's log house is at the front left. Cannon and a gentleman, with his watch chain across his vest, mark the contrast of time and history with timelessness and nature, which permeates the Council Grounds to this day. Letchworth shared with the Iroquois a pervading sense of openness and inclusiveness, a philosophy that fully embraced the ideas of respect and balance in the natural world.

The Council House originally stood at Caneadea on the banks of the upper Genesee River. William Pryor Letchworth (left) and historian John S. Minard (right) were responsible for saving it. Having served the Seneca and their British-Tory allies in the Revolutionary War, the structure fell into ruin following Seneca abandonment of the Caneadea Reservation. At Minard's suggestion, Letchworth shipped it by canal to the Glen Iris Estate for preservation. (Letchworth State Park.)

John Shanks, grandson of Mary Jemison, is shown here beside the Seneca Council House. Letchworth engaged Shanks to rebuild this historic structure using its original layout and logs. The work was completed in 1872 on the Council Grounds. (Letchworth State Park.)

Letchworth placed the Council House on an eminence above the Genesee River prior to his restoration of the denuded landscape. It was constructed about 1780 by Seneca, with the help of British military carpenters dispatched from Fort Niagara. Revolutionary War captive Moses Van Campen ran the gauntlet to the safety of the door of this Council House at Caneadea in 1782.

At the Last Council Fire on the Genesee organized by Letchworth in 1872, the Council House was rededicated. Prominent guests, both Native American and white, gathered for the event. Pictured are former president Millard Fillmore, fifth from the right, and Solomon O'Bail, the grandson of Cornplanter, a great leader of the Iroquois Confederacy, in the center under the point of the canoe. (Letchworth State Park.)

Delegates to the Last Council Fire signed the visitors' register. This extract from the register shows the signatures of several dignitaries including Pres. Millard Fillmore, William Pryor Letchworth, and Augustus Frank, a former U.S. congressman from Warsaw. (Letchworth State Park.)

Appearing in this photograph of the council's Iroquois dignitaries from left to right are James Shongo, son of the Caneadea leader Colonel Shongo; George Jones, "a noted warrior"; William Blacksnake, grandson of Governor Blacksnake; Kate Osborne, granddaughter of Capt. Joseph Brant; W. J. Simcoe Kerr, grandson of Brant and a great-grandson of Sir William Johnson; Nicholson H. Parker, brother of Gen. Ely Parker and a descendant of Red Jacket; Solomon O'Bail; John Jacket, grandson of Red Jacket; and "Buffalo" Tom Jemison, grandson of Mary Jemison. (Letchworth State Park.)

Solomon O'Bail, also known as Ho-way-no-ah, spoke during the council, renewing the ancient ties between the Seneca and Mohawk tribes. Grasping the hand of the Mohawk, Kerr, he stated, "May the remembrance of this day never fade from our minds or the hearts of our descendants." Later O'Bail led the adoption ceremonies on the Glen Iris lawn, giving William Pryor Letchworth the name Hai-wa-ye-is-tah. (Letchworth State Park.)

After the rededication, visitors came to see the famous Caneadea Council House. Here a family poses with Monashasha, the canoe given to Letchworth by Capt. Ebenezer Dorr of Buffalo. Dorr had purchased it from a Native American family that used it to bring their furs to Mackinaw on Lake Superior. (Letchworth State Park.)

. INTERIOR COUNCIL HOUSE .

The Council House interior has changed little since the days the Seneca met here in council to make decisions important to their community. The benches shown were built by John Shanks for the rededication. Mysterious carvings still adorn the interior.

Mary Jemison, with baby Thomas on her back, trekked the Native American trail from Ohio to the Genesee Valley. Caneadea, with its council house, was a stop on her long journey. William Pryor Letchworth commissioned this bronze statue by Henry K. Bush-Brown, as a tribute to this extraordinary woman.

A sarcophagus was prepared for the remains of Mary Jemison and her reburial when, at her family's request, Letchworth had her body returned to the Genesee Valley, where she had lived most of her adult life and raised her family. Both Native Americans and whites participated in the 1874 ceremonies that concluded with the burning of sacred tobacco. (Castile Historical Society.)

A memorial replaced the original gravestone over her final burial spot, and the statue was erected in 1910 to commemorate Mary Jemison's exemplary life. Her extraordinary strength and perseverance led to enduring respect in both white and Native American worlds.

Mary Jemison built this home for her daughter Nancy. According to local folklore, Mary dragged the lumber by means of a tumpline across her forehead from Whaley's sawmill to her lands at Gardeau. This single-household log cabin–style postdates European contact. Ancient Iroquois homes were multifamily bark longhouses.

Nancy's house is shown with a fireplace, a spinning wheel, cooking utensils, and other household items of her time. The notched log ladder to the left is Seneca. It was carved by John Shanks. Since Seneca longhouses and even early cabins had a central smoke-hole and no chimney, this photograph may reflect later white occupation of the cabin.

In this mid-1870s view, the Council House and a small entrance lodge are seen. Visitors are reading the inscription on Mary's original gravestone. Others shade delicate skins from the sun with their umbrellas. Fencing is visible around two of the memorial trees planted as part of the Council House dedication and Last Council Fire ceremonies in 1872. (Mary Jane York.)

As if posed for a painting, tourists are gathered in the rustic viewing pavilion to enjoy the panorama from the elevated Council Grounds. Perched atop its log pillar, a polished sphere afforded viewers a unique perspective of the magnificent scenery and an experience in imaginative reflection.

Genesee Valley Museum on Indian Council House grounds.

William Pryor Letchworth built the fire-proof Genesee Valley Museum on the Council Grounds in 1898. It was a pioneering advance beyond the private cabinets of natural history of the day and was an early effort toward serious studies of Native American culture and the region's natural history.

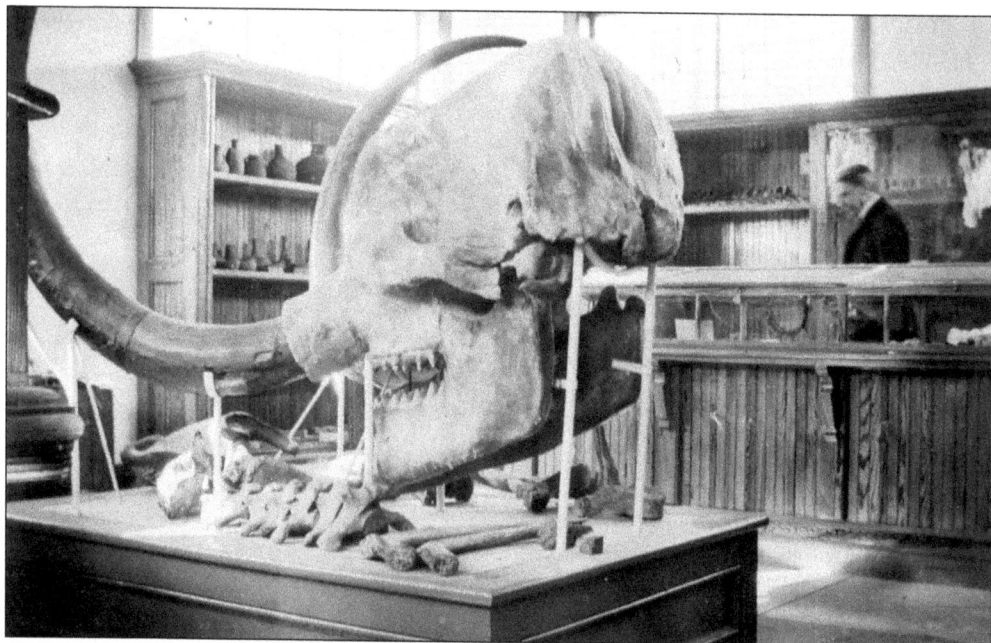

The Genesee Valley Museum showcased a mastodon skull with eight-foot tusks recovered in 1876 in Pike. Large Ice Age mammals lived in western New York until the final retreat of glacial ice, when the Genesee River began cutting the gorges and falls of Letchworth State Park. Henry Howland, seen here, was an early curator and married to Letchworth's cousin Rebecca. He wrote a guidebook to the museum in 1907. (Letchworth State Park.)

Letchworth provided the monument marking Mary Jemison's grave. It was later surmounted with Henry K. Bush-Brown's bronze statue seen today. Years before that, however, this unidentified young woman standing atop the monument anticipated its ultimate adornment. Is this photograph a study in perspective for the sculptor, an art photograph of its day, or was it simply taken on a whim?

Tourism came early and with Letchworth's approval and invitation. Although styles change, peace and happiness are a constant here. The enjoyment of families, friends, and opportunity for renewal of spirit in this peaceful locale remain the same from generation to generation. (Castile Historical Society.)

This massive portion of the legendary Big Tree from Seneca times and Genesee Valley pioneer history was heir to the noble council tree tradition of the Iroquois. However, this section of the Big Tree was thrown into the gorge in the early 20th century as part of changes made that differed from William Pryor Letchworth's inspired, original vision for the Council Grounds. This vision was reestablished in 2006 when a Council Grounds restoration project was completed.

The Council House is shown here flanked by the rustic viewing pavilion and the upper-most section of the famed Big Tree under its protective roof. Letchworth appreciated and sought both protection and access for the unique natural, cultural, and historical treasures of the Genesee Valley.

Four

LOWER FALLS AND WOLF CREEK

Almost a decade before Letchworth arrived, Edward Hunt wrote a letter to landowner George Williams stating, "[The Lower Falls] have thus far to a great extent, escaped the barbarous mutilations which have so nearly obliterated the natural beauty of the Middle Falls. And the earnest petition of good taste, cannot fail to be in every cultivated mind, that the natural beauties of the Lower Falls may never be invaded by the ruthless hand of man. Let no trace of human hands enter that scene of beauty, except such as may be required for facilitating the inspection of its visitors." Hunt's 1851 appeal seemed to work, for the Lower Falls area remained undeveloped and allowed visitors such as *Mr. White, Fishing from Table Rock, Lower Falls* (above) to enjoy the natural splendor of the gorge. (Mary Jane York.)

The wild beauty of the Lower Falls was captured by this engraving and description that appeared in *Picturesque America* in 1874. "A narrow, winding foot-path leads down a steep and rugged defile. Descending this, and guided by the rush of waters below, we suddenly come upon the Lower Falls. Here the waters of the river are gradually led into narrower channels, until the stream becomes a deep-cut canal, which, rushing down in swift current between its narrow limits, widens out just upon the brink of the fall, that more nearly resembles a steep rapid than either of the others. Standing upon one of the projecting rocks which are a feature of this fall, we can only catch occasional glimpses of the cavern's bed, so dense and obscuring are the mist-clouds."

According to Arthur C. Parker's *Skunny Wundy and Other Indian Tales*, the Seneca called the Lower Falls Gahneegattah (Gah-nee-gat-tah). It was here, they said, that the Creator made the home of the Drum Dancers (Jungies), who were instructed to "forever guard the fruits and the fields of grain . . . Upon you depends the growth of the food plants; guard them so my Ongwe [people] may never go hungry."

When the renowned geologist James Hall visited the gorge in the early 1840s, his wife sketched the Lower Falls. In the days of the Seneca, Gahneegattah dropped 90 feet over Table Rock, the large flat rock shelf seen at the center of the sketch. Sugar Loaf rock is to the left of the falls.

These photographs were taken about 30 years after the James Hall sketch was made. The falls have receded through the narrow chute known as the flume. The main falls was now at the head of flume as shown in the upper image. The bottom image was taken above the falls looking down through the flume. All the waters of the Genesee River had to pass through this "deep cut canal."

Above the flume, two smaller falls had formed, one near the head of the flume where the tourists are standing, the other farther upstream near the bend in the gorge. This stereo view image was taken in the 1880s. Within a few generations, the Lower Falls underwent significant changes.

The physical changes were due to the combination of natural and human forces. The waters of the Genesee River continued to sculpt the riverbed while workers in the 1930s removed much of the flume's eastern bank to make way for the Lower Falls Footbridge Trail. It is interesting to compare this 1954 photograph (below) with the one on the top of page 62. A visit to the modern Lower Falls will show even more change. (Letchworth State Park.)

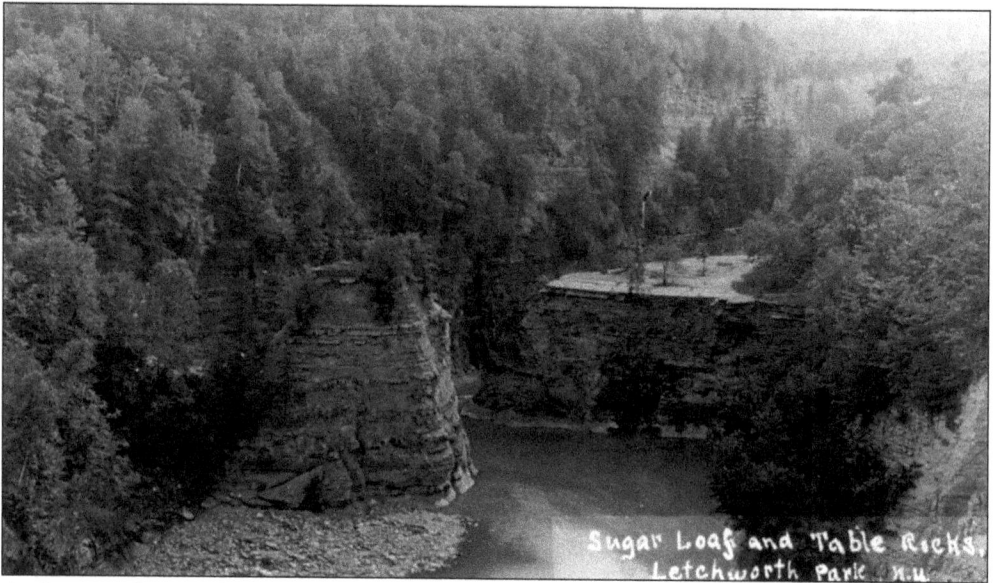

A photographer in the 1860s stated that the Lower Falls, along with Sugar Loaf and Table Rock, "form a wild and picturesque scene rarely surpassed." The postcard above shows the two landmarks around 1920. It is interesting to compare this view with the sketch on page 61. The stereo view image below from the 1860s shows Sugar Loaf, which was also known as Cathedral Rock in William Pryor Letchworth's time.

Adventurous visitors have climbed Sugar Loaf in this stereo view by M. N. Crocker of Perry. A close look shows a daredevil in the top of the tree. This view was taken from the top of the cliff downstream from the falls. Table Rock is to the right; the flume is to the left.

These tourists must have entered the gorge downstream and walked to this rocky bank, for there was no other way to reach the spot where they are posing. Behind them is the face of Table Rock. A century or so earlier, the Lower Falls would have provided a fine background to this 1900 photograph.

Table Rock was popular with visitors and, like today, could be reached by trails cut for that purpose. But the bank is steep and the walking strenuous. Imagine doing it on a hot summer day in late-19th-century fashions. In this undated photograph from the late 1800s, a group of local folks from nearby Castile are posed on Table Rock with the top of the Sugar Loaf behind them. They seem to be enjoying a variety of sports, including croquet, archery, hunting, and

humor. Note the man in the bonnet and the couple who have switched roles. He is carrying the umbrella, and she is proudly displaying a rifle. Luckily for this active crowd, the cold waters of Shongo Spring trickled down the bank not far from where they were standing so they were able to quench their thirst. (Castile Historical Society.)

Some day / perhaps / I will / see Portage / again

Remember me to all my friends

What a pleasant / day and trip it / was. Often / recall it

Swift. / Beautiful / Water

N.Y. State is home to me.

Portage Falls

Others who came saw the Lower Falls in a more contemplative way. In a poem titled *The Lower Falls of the Upper Genesee at Midnight*, Jerome Stillson described the sound of the falls as "grand cathedral music" and wrote, "I bow and shrink to nothingness amid the awful grandeur of the place; Truly God is here!" The writer of this 1905 postcard was also clearly moved by her visit.

An unidentified man stands at the edge of Table Rock enjoying the beauty of the gorge. Beyond him, the Genesee River flows away from the last of the three falls of Sehgahunda into a broader valley that is more hospitable for settled life. Lee's Landing, with its fertile soil and trees, is around the far bend.

This map shows the river from Upper Falls to Big Bend. Below the Lower Falls, the gorge opens for about a mile and a half into a wide valley that attracted settlers. Prospect Home and Chestnut Lawn, originally owned by Reuben and Perry Jones, became tenant farms owned by William Pryor Letchworth. The home of H. Lee marks Lee's Landing, shown in the photograph on page 70.

According to Mildred Lee Hills Anderson, who grew up at Lee's Landing, this was an early major river crossing known as Roger's Bridge. This early-1900s photograph of Lee's Landing (above) was taken from the east bank of the Genesee River, looking west. The Lee farm is in the center of the image, and the road leading up the bank is still in use today. The flat land above is the area where the Lower Falls pool is located. The bottom photograph shows the farms on the east side of the river. The road leads to the homes and school on Big Bend and is still in use in Letchworth State Park. Big Bend, sometimes called Great Bend, lies downstream from Lee's Landing and is the deepest part of the gorge in Letchworth.

The 1920s postcard (above) and the 1860s stereo view image capture the grandeur of the Big Bend gorge. According to William Cullen Bryant's *Picturesque America*, "To the tourist who is possessed of a full measure of courage and strength, a journey along the river's shore from the lower falls to the valley will reveal wonders of natural architecture hardly exceeded by the canyons of the far West. Here, hidden beneath the shadows of the overhanging walls of rock, it is hard to imagine that, just beyond that line of Norway pines that forms a fringe against the sky above, lie fertile fields and quiet homes."

Wolf Creek enters the Genesee Valley below Big Bend. The stream was named in pioneer days when wolves were found throughout the valley. Since they endangered the settlers' livestock, local officials offered a $5 bounty for the "ears and scalp" of wolves. This log bridge over Wolf Creek was probably built before 1830. By that time, the wolves were gone, but the name remains.

As Wolf Creek approaches the gorge, it cascades 225 feet down a narrow ravine. The early road that crossed the Wolf Creek Bridge is seen at the top of the image.

In the late 1800s, the easiest access to Wolf Creek falls was by water. To capture this final cascade in the creek, the photographer and his assistant have probably traveled upstream from nearby St. Helena by small boat.

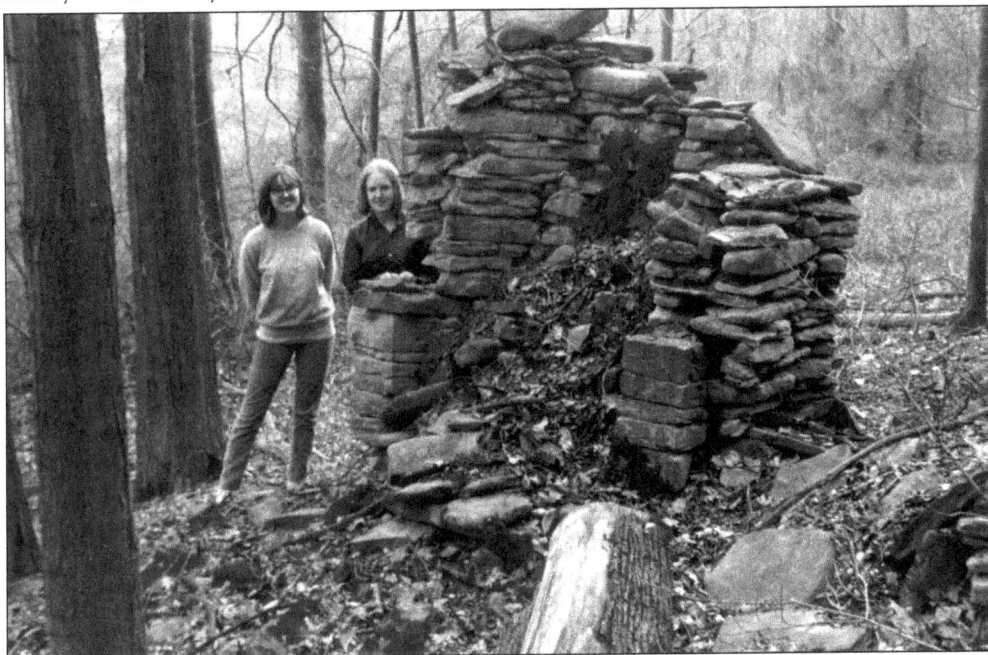

Christine DeGolyer (left) and Ruth Lee DeGolyer Hackett stand by the ruins of a sawmill near the mouth of Wolf Creek in 1967. Mary Jemison's sons were working for the mill's owner when John Jemison killed his brother Jesse in 1812. A grieving Mary carried her son back to Gardeau for burial. Since this photograph was taken, floodwaters have erased most traces of the mill. (Castile Historical Society.)

Just north of Wolf Creek in the modern park is the Tea Table Rock area, named for an unusual rock formation. This 1920s photograph is believed to show the "table" high on the edge of the cliff just below the last two small trees. Some local residents still remember the adventure of climbing onto the "tea table." The natural formation fell into the gorge around 1950. (Letchworth State Park.)

A solitary figure stands on the bank of the Genesee River at Wolf Creek. Here the river, after winding through the Portage and Big Bend gorges, enters the Gardeau Valley, whose fertile flats attracted settlers for thousands of years.

Five

VANISHED VILLAGES

Beyond Big Bend and Wolf Creek, the valley widens. This begins the area of the park where community life once flourished. The first were the small, seasonal fishing camps prehistoric people built along the Genesee River for thousands of years, followed later by the Seneca village of Ga-da-oh. That was followed by pioneer families, who also established bustling villages here. All are now vanished from the valley. Shown in this stereo view is an early cabin along the Genesee River. Although the exact location is not known, it represents settled life in the valley. Stump fences such as these can still be seen in the park. (Letchworth State Park.)

The Gardeau Valley stretches over six miles along the Genesee River. It is a broad, flat valley with deep, fertile soils deposited by countless spring floods. The hills were covered by forests with abundant plants and animals. The Seneca knew it as Ga-da-oh, or "the bank in front," and once had a flourishing village in the area shown in this engraving. Two runaway black slaves

were living in cabins at Gardeau when Mary Jemison and her children arrived in 1779. This engraving is taken from the sixth edition of *A Narrative of the Life of Mary Jemison* by James Seaver, which was edited by William Pryor Letchworth in 1898.

Where the GENESEE enters the GARDEAU DIVIDE,
Gardeau Reservation Near Perry N.Y.

Mary Jemison described Gardeau Valley as mostly open flats. The Senecas knew that others had lived in the beautiful valley before them. Evidence of these "old ones," the prehistoric occupants of the area, was found by archaeologists near St. Helena in the 1930s. This image shows what is known as the Gardeau Divide at the north end of the valley.

This statue of Mary Jemison stands in the Buchanan Valley, near Gettysburg, Pennsylvania, where the young Scotch-Irish Colonial girl was captured by a raiding party of French and Shawnee in 1758. Adopted by the Seneca as Dehgewanus, she lived for several years along the Ohio River, later coming to live along the Genesee River. She came to Gardeau with her children when the Sullivan Expedition destroyed her village in 1779.

Varⁿ at Gardeau. 1.35 West
Septr 6th 1798.

Gardeau was one of the reservations established at the Treaty of Big Tree in 1797. This old map shows the reservation with a group of cabins belonging to Mary Jemison, the "White Woman on Gardeau." The clustering of the cabins kept the extended Seneca family together as the ancient longhouse had done generations before.

This cabin, one of the structures shown on the old Gardeau map, was said to have been constructed by Mary Jemison for her daughter Nancy. Eventually it became the home of white families and later was donated to William Pryor Letchworth by John Olmsted. It now stands on the Council Grounds.

This image from a stereo view made by George Washburn of Castile is titled *Gardeau, –Mary Jemison's Home on Her Reservation*. It is believed that the Jemison cabin was located in the distance, but changes in the course of the river make the actual location difficult to determine. The roadway in the foreground came north from St. Helena.

The "Old White Woman" was a common sight in the valley throughout the pioneer period. Local families still tell of her visits to their pioneer ancestors, and there are many stories of how hungry settlers and weary travelers found food and shelter in her home. In the fall of 1823, she walked four miles to an interview with Dr. James Seaver. The narrative, published a year later, preserved a life story that Letchworth described as being, "so extraordinary as to seem unreal." The image above shows an aged Mary Jemison as she might have looked in 1831 when the Jemisons became the last Seneca to leave the Genesee Valley. She moved from Gardeau to the Buffalo Creek Reservation near Buffalo in 1831 and died there in 1833 at age 90. (Mary Jane York.)

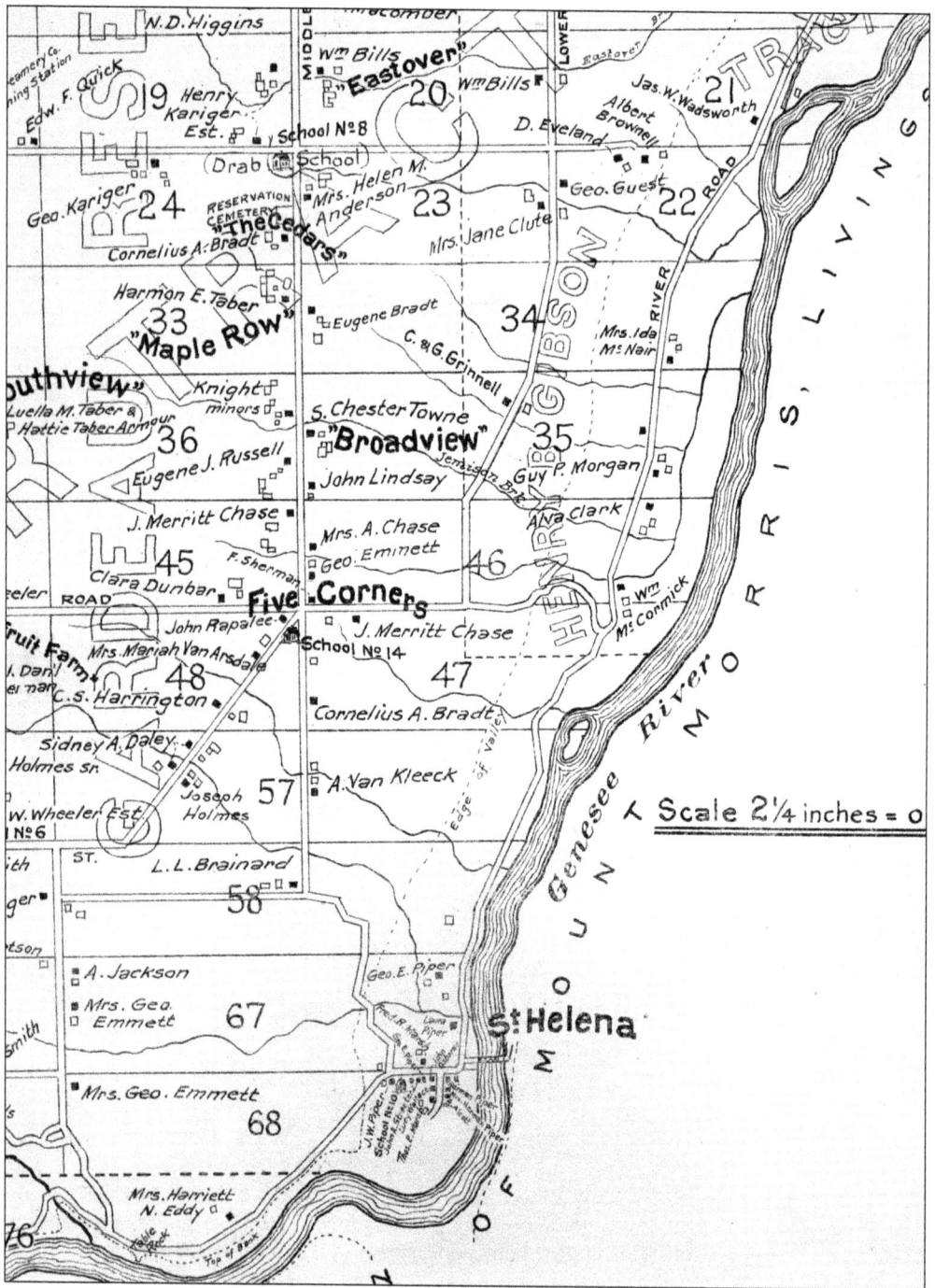

This 1903 map shows the Genesee River valley in the town of Castile in Wyoming County and the community of St. Helena. The town was settled in the 1820s by pioneers attracted by the waterpower, fertile flats, and abundant timber. St. Helena was connected to neighboring communities by several roads. One important road that followed the river to Smokey Hollow lay east of the present Letchworth State Park road.

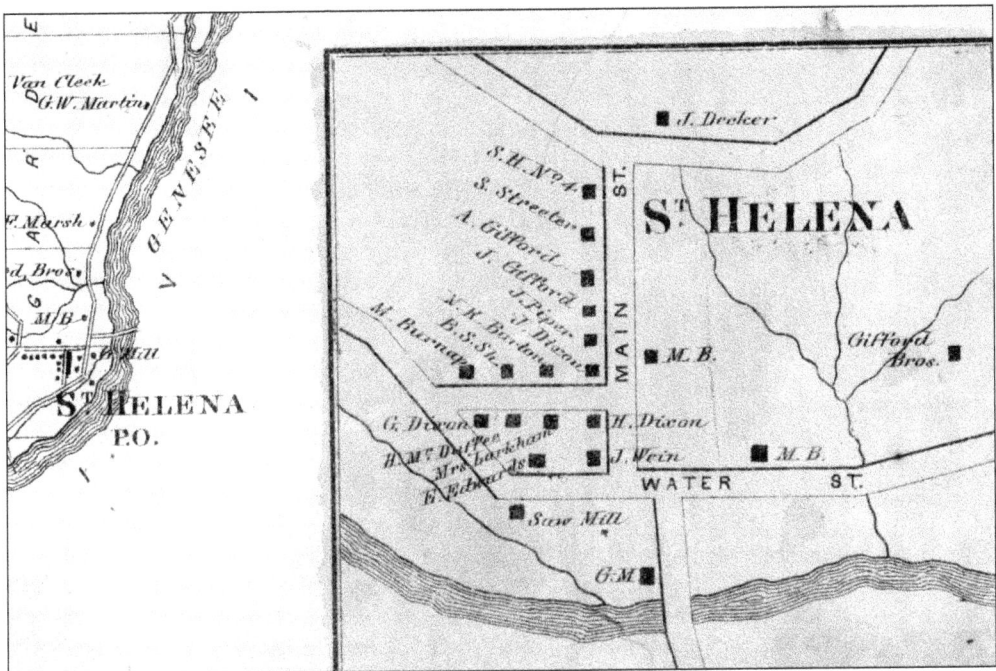

A newspaper article in the *Nunda News* in 1920 described St. Helena of 1860 as "one of the prosperous hamlets along the river, with a flour mill, two sawmills, shingle mill, paper mill, and two general stores, a hotel and 25 dwellings, with a school having 75 pupils during the winter term." This St. Helena map is from an 1866 atlas.

This photograph, looking from the west bank toward the river, shows St. Helena surrounded by the rich farmland that drew settlers to the area. The prominent white building is the school. Constructed in 1856, it replaced a smaller edifice. The new schoolhouse reflected a growing enrollment and the importance the residents placed on education. (Castile Historical Society.)

This undated image shows Milton Burnap and his family on Maiden Lane in St. Helena. Burnap served in the Civil War in Company D of 136th New York, one of two regiments that trained at Camp Williams, now the park's parade grounds. He later ran a cider mill in the village. Floods were a constant threat, and this house was once moved over 300 feet by rushing waters. (Castile Historic Society.)

Pictured here is a denizen of St. Helena, who must have been of some importance to have his image preserved over the years. The wagons and cultivator beside the barn were mainstays of 19th-century farming. (Castile Historical Society.)

This early photograph is labeled "Mr. Piper." Herman Piper is one of the many members of the Piper family that settled in St. Helena. The bowed handle to his left is a scythe. He probably deserved a rest if he had been scything very long harvesting grain. Piper was also employed by the U.S. Geological Survey to read and report water levels in the government gauge on the St. Helena bridge. (Castile Historical Society.)

This photograph shows the St. Helena school prior to 1920 when it was sold and demolished. The bell was a favorite of the residents as it echoed through the valley calling area children to school. The individuals, from left to right, are Calvin Burnap Jr., Glen Streeter, possibly teacher Ruth Phelps, George Streeter, and Virginia Teeple. (Castile Historical Society.)

This view shows a road in the late 1800s. Travel on this road was a necessity to go between St. Helena and the Gardeau area or to visit other farms along the river. Rain, snow, and ice in the winter made such travel dangerous and contributed to the isolation of people in the valley. (Castile Historical Society.)

This bridge across the river at St. Helena was the most substantial erected at this site. Former wooden structures were washed out when ice broke up in the spring. This bridge was removed in 1950 during the construction of the Mount Morris dam. (Castile Historical Society.)

By the time of this 1940s aerial view of St. Helena, the village had vanished. All that remains is the St. Helena bridge and two homes that existed until 1948. The road system on the west (left) appears to be intact. The land was still used by area farmers well after most residents left. Much of the land was purchased by Rochester Gas and Electric Corporation for a proposed power project in the Mount Morris Highbanks area. (Letchworth State Park.)

North of St. Helena and Gardeau was a place where a few farms dotted the valley flats and hillsides. This part of Letchworth State Park is still referred to as Smoky (or Smokey) Hollow, because the valley here has a tendency to fill with mist on chilly, fall mornings. In the distance are the first cliffs that mark the beginning of the Mount Morris Highbanks.

Farming in the 19th century was not easy, but with the strong families and a network of neighbors, farming and farm life flourished. Two members of the Barager family of nearby Portage are shown working in their hay field in the early 1900s. Such scenes were common throughout the Genesee Valley. (Portage Town Historian and Livingston County Historian's Office.)

Smokey Hollow was not a formal village. Only a few farm families lived in the area, including the Walter Chafee family, shown here in a postcard from around 1915. The young woman wearing the hat was Edna Hewitt from Portage, who boarded with the Chafee family.

Hewitt was the teacher of the one-room schoolhouse at Smokey Hollow. Here she proudly stands before what was known as the Littledyke School. Perhaps the most modern and best-equipped school of its day was Genesee Falls No. 2, planned and built by William Pryor Letchworth. A replica of the Letchworth school stands on Trout Pond Road.

The Silver Lake Outlet flows into the Genesee River north of Smokey Hollow and Kissel Point. As it nears the deepening valley, the stream tumbles over a series of rapids and waterfalls as shown in this 1870s stereo view image. Before 1800, settlers began to tap the outlet's power to run their mills, eventually creating the village of Gibsonville.

It is no surprise that the largest building in Gibsonville was a mill. Shown here is the impressive mill owned by George T. West. Originally built as a gristmill, it was converted to a paper mill in 1840. It burned in 1894.

This map from the 1872 Livingston County atlas shows Gibsonville with its road network and several houses. A listing from four years earlier included the paper mill, a school, a blacksmith, a store, a shoemaker, and a justice of the peace. The undated photograph below shows the Gibsonville Post Office with unidentified townspeople. Within 30 years, the village had dwindled to 17 property owners with one of those being Rochester Gas and Electric Corporation. (Livingston County Historian's Office.)

The farm economy began to improve with the arrival of the machine. This is an early Buffalo Pitts 10-horsepower threshing machine owned by Walter Hull of Gibsonville. People shown from left to right are Ray Matteson, Walter Hull, Earl Paddock, Kate Hull Hare, and Earl Waters. Steam-powered machines of this kind were moved from farm to farm at harvest time. (Livingston County Historian's Office.)

This stereo view shows the last of the remarkable geographic features that set the park area apart from the rest of western New York. Here the river enters the Mount Morris Highbanks, the last of the Genesee's gorges in Letchworth State Park.

Six

HIGHBANKS AND THE MODERN PARK

This 1874 engraving from *Picturesque America* shows a lone fisherman launching his boat into the Genesee River. Beyond him rise the cliffs of what is known to this day as the Highbanks. The Mount Morris Highbanks is a canyon about seven miles long with cliffs reaching 300 feet above the river. Their natural beauty and abundant resources have drawn people for centuries. Many generations of native people built their villages upon the banks and farmed the fertile flats within the gorge, followed by the pioneers and their descendants. The Highbanks also symbolize the development and expansion of Letchworth State Park through the 20th century.

High Banks, Mount Morris.

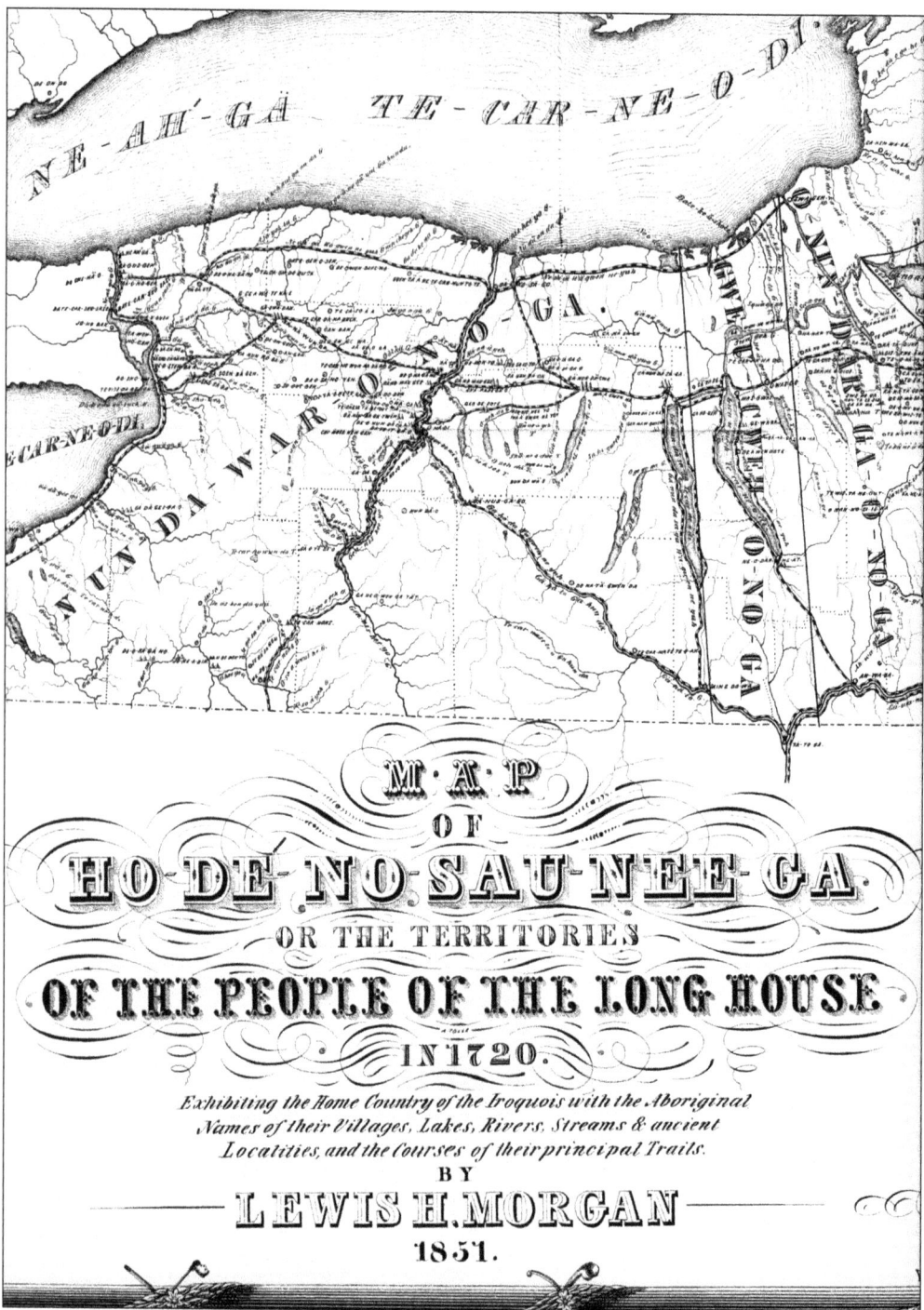

This Seneca portion of the *Map of Ho-de-no-sau-nee-ga or the Territories of the People of the Long House in 1720,* was published in Lewis Henry Morgan's landmark *League of the Iroquois* in Rochester in 1851. Villages, trails, and landmarks of the Seneca-Iroquois, "Keepers of the Western Door" of the famed Iroquois Confederacy, are shown on the map.

This map of Squawkie Hill shows an area at the very edge of the Genesee Valley where the Seneca had a lively village and farms into the early 19th century. Ceremonial mounds of the "old ones" from many centuries earlier, now gone, were located near here. *Squawkie* refers to the Musquawkie or Fox Indians, who had a refugee settlement here and were absorbed into Seneca life. The lands were set aside at the Big Tree Treaty in 1797 and sold in 1826.

This is Shoh-son-do-want, better known as "Buffalo" Tom Jemison. He was grandson of Mary Jemison and the son of Thomas, the baby depicted in the cradleboard on the Mary Jemison statue at the Council Grounds. Born around 1795, Tom died at Cattaraugus in 1878. He lived for many years at Squawkie Hill. (Letchworth State Park.)

Tom Jemison built this cabin in the early 1800s. It is located on the Squawkie Hill map under the name of a later occupant, Mrs. Ayrault. It stood until the 1960s, perhaps one of the last Native American–built structures remaining in the east. Salvaged by Gabe Judkins and Ted Bartlett, the cabin's remains are preserved for future research in Letchworth State Park. (Livingston County Historian's Office.)

Apples were a favorite of the Seneca and early descriptions of their villages often mention extensive orchards. The Seneca used apples in several ways, including baking them in hot ashes and making sauces. Apples were stored in barrels or dried to preserve them. Although many of these orchards were destroyed in the Revolutionary War, some marked village sites for generations to come, as do these apple trees said to have been planted by Mary Jemison. (Livingston County Historian's Office.)

Famous scientist and explorer of the Colorado River John Wesley Powell was born in Mount Morris in 1834. Powell saw his first grand canyon at these Highbanks. This area became an important destination for tourists like the gentleman in this 1870s view. Little did he know that within a century, a mighty dam would stand in the gorge and where he was sitting would be a modern state park.

This map was prepared by John S. Minard for William Pryor Letchworth in 1907, just after the Glen Iris Estate became Letchworth State Park. The map was adapted by the engineers of the New York State Water Commission in 1908 to show how a proposed power dam just above the village of Portageville would be placed to form a lake to the south. The project was defeated and changes in the park boundaries were soon underway. Letchworth State Park reached the Mount Morris Highbanks within four decades.

After Letchworth's death, the American Scenic and Historic Preservation Society began development of the new public park. The greatest challenge was to take a private estate and change it into a park that could accommodate a modern visitor. These old, outdated estate gates, south of Glen Iris, would not suffice for the new century. (Letchworth State Park.)

As shown in this 1920s photograph, even the width of the main estate gates near Dehgayasoh Creek could not accommodate two-way traffic. If Letchworth State Park was to flourish, it had to deal with the automobile. (Letchworth State Park.)

The automobile was changing America, and Letchworth State Park was no exception. This real-photo postcard is labeled "Dinner Time—Letchworth, July 28, 1912." As the number of automobiles grew, so did the dangers on the unimproved roads. In 1917, the automobile shown in the photograph below plunged over the cliffs below the Portage bridge, killing two young women.

Scene of Accident at Letchworth Park

Some of the earliest roadwork took place at what became the Portageville entrance to the park. The old estate road was extended to the south and others were widened and eventually paved. New stone gates welcomed visitors to the growing park. (Letchworth State Park.)

The new park road carried visitors under the bridge to the Middle and Upper Falls area and to the new Glen Iris Inn. As this image shows, stone walls were built by park employees to resemble the early stone work William Pryor Letchworth had constructed throughout his estate. (Letchworth State Park.)

Parking lots were among the earliest additions to the park. This 1920s photograph shows one of the first parking areas near the Middle and Upper Falls. This parking area is still in use today. (Letchworth State Park.)

Glen Iris, William Pryor Letchworth's private residence, opened as an inn in May 1914. This 1915 postcard shows the early dining room. Many of the dishes in the cupboard, the artwork, and other furnishing probably belonged to Letchworth. Dinners were offered for $1. The electric lights used in Glen Iris were powered by gasoline generators.

Maintaining the park called for more workers and equipment. This multiple-bay garage was constructed at the base of the hill below the Council Grounds in 1928 for use by park workforces. The Prospect Home farmhouse became the labor center where park workers lived. (Letchworth State Park.)

The same building was later modified to meet a growing public demand for overnight accommodations. The structure became Pinewood Lodge after the garage units were made into motel-style rooms, complete with kitchens, baths, and sleeping areas. (Letchworth State Park.)

The park museum, shown under construction, opened in 1913 to provide educational experiences for park visitors. The building is of tile construction, faced with stone from the riverbed. Built on the site of the formal gardens, it replaced the original museum located at the Council Grounds. To the right of the new structure is William Pryor Letchworth's icehouse.

Posed on the lawn in front of the vine-covered museum, the Arthur and Margaret Allen family of Rochester enjoys a day in the park around 1932. Like many visitors to Letchworth, young Margaret Allen (Cook) kneeling next to her brother Art, would have a lifelong love of Letchworth State Park. (Cook family.)

The increasing number of visitors also caused a demand for picnic shelters, benches, and comfort stations. A Sunday school group from nearby Hunt poses in front of the Middle Falls comfort station built around 1914. This comfort station is still in use and may be one of the earliest restrooms in the state park system.

Letchworth Park Camping Grounds

The first overnight campgrounds in the park opened in 1923 at the Lower Falls, near present-day Cabin Area B. Overnight and extended stays in the park became popular at this time. Cabins replaced these tents a decade later.

Stairs and ornamental railings as seen here were built on the Glen Iris Estate to assist the public in gaining access to steep areas. Note the round timbers used with branches woven in for added strength and beauty. This rustic design was in keeping with the vision of William Webster, the landscape architect who designed the original estate. (Letchworth State Park.)

Later stairways were more functional than artistic. This 1920s photograph shows workmen constructing a stairway out of square-sawn timber along a steep cliff near the Lower Falls. These were later replaced by stone stairs. (Letchworth State Park.)

Patterned on William Pryor Letchworth's efforts to replant the once-wooded slopes, a forest arboretum was established in 1912. Stands of the same species of trees were planted to study the growth in forest conditions. Pictured here is a block in the arboretum area near Inspiration Point being thinned to encourage growth of the healthiest trees. Many of these trees still stand in their original arboretum blocks. (Letchworth State Park.)

This 1920s photograph shows a team of horses hitched to a log sled in the log yard of the park sawmill. Behind the park worker are logs piled in a bunk, ready to be milled into boards. Most of the lumber used in the park construction projects came from trees killed by the chestnut blight. The sawmill is still used today. (Letchworth State Park.)

The photograph above shows the early stages of construction of the Dehgayasoh Creek bridge in 1927. The work crew is building forms for the foundation of the bridge that will be filled with concrete. Next a concrete arch will be formed and poured. A later stage is shown below where the arch is formed and earth fill is being added to provide a base for the concrete bridge deck that will be placed across the opening between the stonewalls on the sides of the structure. Many bridges in the park are concrete cores faced with stone. Dehgayasoh Bridge is still in use today. (Letchworth State Park.)

As the park expanded north, so did the roads. Workmen are shown here in 1930 sorting stone to face the concrete wall on the side of the main road at Wolf Creek. Teams of horses are seen working on the bank. (Letchworth State Park.)

This winter scene shows the completed stonework at Wolf Creek hill that enhanced even a snowy drive through Letchworth State Park. As the Great Depression deepened, the park became more dependent on public works programs to carry out needed construction. The work at Wolf Creek was one of these projects. (Letchworth State Park.)

Although the Great Depression paralyzed the United States during the 1930s, state and federal public works programs advanced construction and conservation work in the park. The most famous of these was the New Deal program known as the Civilian Conservation Corps (CCC). One of the great accomplishments of the program was the construction of the Lower Falls footbridge. (Letchworth State Park.)

At the program's peak, four CCC camps were in operation in Letchworth State Park. Each held 200 men, with additional administrative and support personnel. According to park officials, this conservation army accomplished in one year what normally would have taken 10 years to complete. (Castile Historical Society.)

Several thousand men participated in the CCC in Letchworth State Park between 1933 and 1941. They were young and came from a variety of places and all walks of life, but shared a need for work and a willingness to learn. The men shown here from St. Helena Camp No. 76 left the program with new skills and pride in a job well done. Among these CCC boys is Edward James Reid (middle row, fourth from right). (Reid family.)

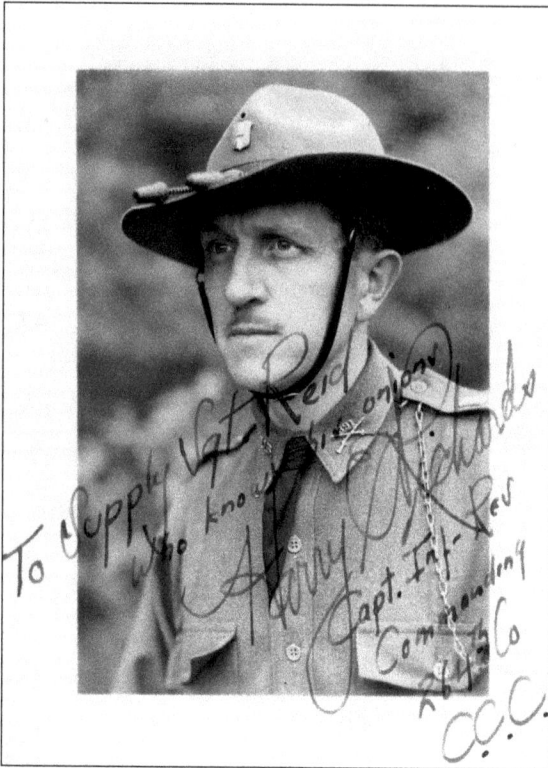

The camps were run by regular or reserve U.S. Army officers in a military manner, although the work projects were supervised by civilian foremen. Since many of the CCC members entered the service in World War II, this experience was their first taste of army-style life. This photograph was given to St. Helena supply sergeant Edward Reid by his camp commander Harry Richards. (Reid family.)

Edward Reid, born in Nebraska, came to the St. Helena camp in 1934. Recruits at Letchworth came from all over the country. They earned $30 a month, most of which was sent home to their families. The money spent on supplies by the camps and by CCC men on weekends benefited the local towns. (Reid family.)

As the camp's supply sergeant, Reid was assigned to the building shown here. The government provided uniforms, work clothing, and tools. Most CCC veterans especially remember the food, since it was more plentiful than what was available back home. The sign above the shelves reads "Remember; it fits someone." (Reid family.)

The St. Helena camp opened on the bluff west of the vanished village in May 1934. Although it was only in operation for two years, camp members built miles of roads, cut 15 miles of trails, built a parking lot, water lines, a comfort station, a shelter, water fountains, 13 fireplaces, and 26 stone tables. (Reid family.)

The Big Bend camp was the first of the Letchworth camps, established on June 19, 1933. In a 30-month period, the camp built six miles of roads, laid electric, phone, water, and sewer lines, built Cabin Area E, the parade ground's log shelter, and did an impressive amount of conservation work. The camp was later used as a works project camp and closed in August 1942.

The Gibsonville camp was set up in September 1933 and operated for four years. In addition to constructing the main road from Mount Morris to Wolf Creek, the men built Kissel Point picnic area, Cabin Area C, and operated a quarry. During World War II, refugees from Hungary were housed in the camp buildings. Chimneys from the Gibsonville and Big Bend camps can still be seen in the park. (Castile Historical Society.)

The men of the Lower Falls camp No. 49, which was set up in May 1935, worked from Gardeau to Lower Falls, building parking lots, roads, stairs, walls, and much of present day Cabin Area B. They were also responsible for the trails to the Lower Falls and improving the old trail between the falls and Inspiration Point. Their most lasting accomplishment was the Lower Falls footbridge. (Castile Historical Society.)

The Lower Falls camp was closed in October 1941, but the buildings were left standing. From 1944 to 1946 they housed up to 200 German prisoners of war. Photographs of the camp have not yet been found, perhaps because the park was closed due to gasoline rationing. This sign hung in the prison camp at Lower Falls. (Photograph by Gerald Barkley, Nunda Historical Society.)

Because of the labor shortage, German prisoners worked on area farms and in factories. Many became acquainted with local residents and the Letchworth State Park area. One prisoner of war painted this watercolor of the statue of Mary Jemison and gave it to the Davis family. The name of the soldier has been lost. (Castile Historical Society.)

This letter was found in the barracks at Lower Falls after the Germans were repatriated in 1946. The letter was written in September 1944 by a German mother to her son Arnfried. In it she told her son to "stay healthy and think about the future." The Lower Falls of the Genesee River must have seemed a long way from home to the prisoner of war.

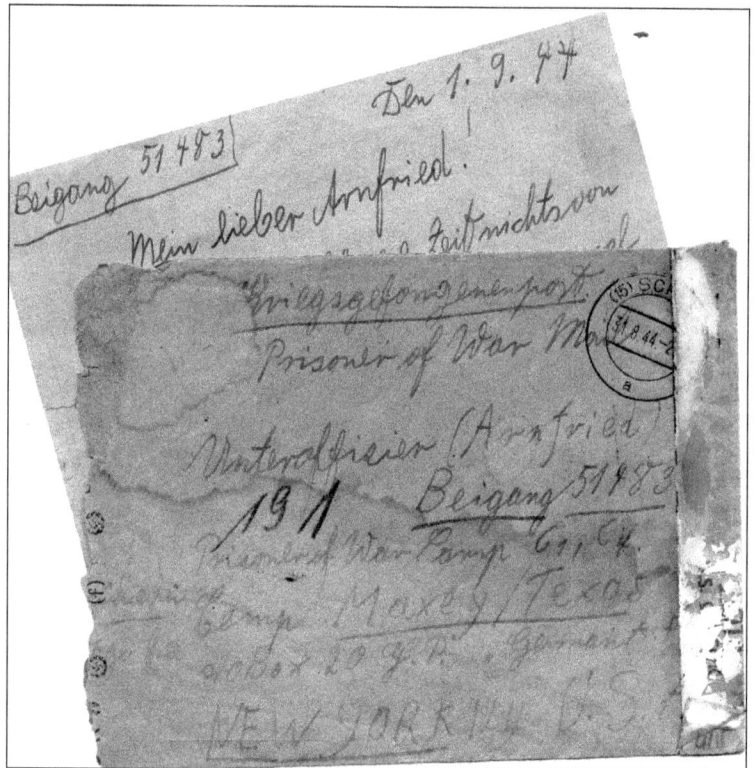

116

Even before World War II, there was a push for more recreational opportunities at Letchworth State Park. A field just inside the Castile entrance became the Archery Field, a name still used today. Archery competitions were frequently held and targets were available until the 1960s. Local schools, colleges, and community organizations also used the field for pageants and field days. (Letchworth State Park.)

The swimming pool at Lower Falls near the former site of the CCC camp was drawing large crowds of swimmers by August 1950. Letchworth State Park, at this time, consisted of a little more than 7,000 acres. Within 10 years, the park doubled in size as it completed its expansion through the valley. (Letchworth State Park.)

High Banks of Genesee River, near M

The greatest 20th-century engineering feat in the Genesee Valley took place in the Highbanks area, shown here in the 1930s. There had been talk of building a flood control and power-generating dam at Highbanks as early as the 1890s, and the Rochester Gas and Electric Corporation acquired land to Wolf Creek in the 1920s and 1930s with the expectation of a Highbanks dam.

The Army Corps of Engineers oversaw the project. Work began in early 1948 with the construction of a cofferdam in the ancient riverbed. Both the riverbed and cliff walls had to be prepared before work on the massive concrete structure could begin. (Weir family.)

Here the outer layers of the cliff wall have been excavated and the dam begins to take shape. Private contracting firms under the supervision of the Army Corp of Engineers did the work. Nearly 500 workers were hired for the project, many of them young men from nearby towns looking for good-paying jobs. (Photograph by John Weaver, Nunda Historical Society.)

Robert E. Weir Jr. was a 22-year-old war veteran who worked on the project for three years, earning $1.67 per hour. He is shown here with his crew preparing to release concrete from a 22-ton bucket. With each pour raising one section of the dam about three and half feet, it took four years of constant work to reach its full height of 246 feet. (Weir family.)

The work site was hot and often dangerous. Robert E. Weir Jr. and eight members of his pouring crew were nearly killed when the giant bucket fell from 300 feet in the air. There were injuries on the project, but only one person was killed in a fall from the bank. Despite the sometimes difficult working conditions, Weir considered it "an experience of a lifetime." (Livingston County Historian's Office.)

The Mount Morris Dam was completed in May 1952 at a cost of $19.8 million, $400,000 under its original estimate. The total height of the dam is 246 feet, and it is 221 feet thick. At 1,026 feet long with 750,000 cubic feet of concrete, it is the largest concrete gravity dam east of the Mississippi River. (Livingston County Historians Office.)

It was estimated that by 1960, the dam had already prevented $8 million in flood damage downstream. Several floods have challenged the Mount Morris Dam since, almost filling it to capacity. Shown above is the dam holding back floodwaters in the 1960s. In 1972, Hurricane Agnes brought the waters even higher, but the dam held, creating a huge lake that flooded the Gardeau Flats, shown below.

The aerial view of the Highbanks area looks east toward the Genesee Valley. The construction seen near the center of the photograph marks the site of the Highbanks Recreation Area that opened in the 1960s. The facility, shown soon after completion in the second photograph, became a symbol of the new demands of the modern park visitor. The Highbanks Recreation Area includes the Olympic-sized Gordon W. Harvey swimming pool, a parking area, picnic shelters, and other facilities. Since the facility was built, the park has continued to change and grow. What remains constant is the commitment to goals established over a century ago when William Pryor Letchworth gave the original lands to the State of New York. (Letchworth State Park.)

This early-1900s photograph shows a dam across the Genesee River near Mount Morris below Letchworth State Park. The original plan was to build an aqueduct similar to the one in Portageville to carry the Genesee Valley Canal across the Genesee River. To save money, a dam was built and canal boats moved across the river to a lock on the far bank. Later electric power was generated at this spot. (Livingston County Historian's Office.)

In the distance, the Genesee River reenters its preglacial valley. The river's journey from the Portage gorge is long, both in miles and years. That journey, and the natural and human forces that shaped it, created the special place known as Letchworth State Park.

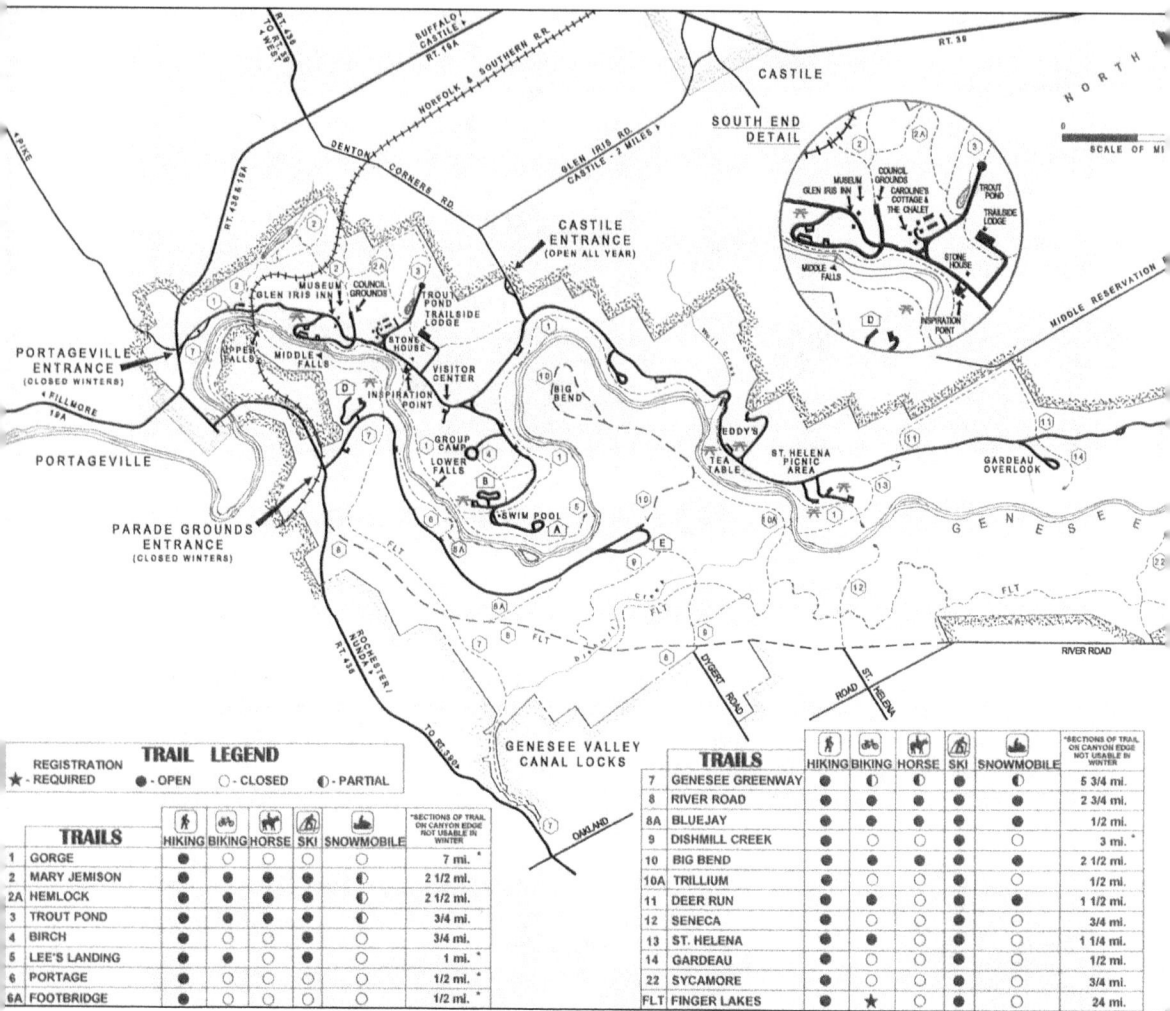

TRAIL LEGEND

REGISTRATION ★ - REQUIRED

● - OPEN ○ - CLOSED ◐ - PARTIAL

	TRAILS	HIKING	BIKING	HORSE	SKI	SNOWMOBILE	*SECTIONS OF TRAIL ON CANYON EDGE NOT USABLE IN WINTER
1	GORGE	●	○	○	●	○	7 mi. *
2	MARY JEMISON	●	●	●	●	◐	2 1/2 mi.
2A	HEMLOCK	●	●	●	●	◐	2 1/2 mi.
3	TROUT POND	●	●	●	●	◐	3/4 mi.
4	BIRCH	●	○	○	●	○	3/4 mi.
5	LEE'S LANDING	●	●	○	●	○	1 mi. *
6	PORTAGE	●	○	○	○	○	1/2 mi. *
6A	FOOTBRIDGE	●	○	○	○	○	1/2 mi. *

	TRAILS	HIKING	BIKING	HORSE	SKI	SNOWMOBILE	*SECTIONS OF TRAIL ON CANYON EDGE NOT USABLE IN WINTER
7	GENESEE GREENWAY	●	◐	◐	●	◐	5 3/4 mi.
8	RIVER ROAD	●	●	●	●	●	2 3/4 mi.
8A	BLUEJAY	●	●	●	●	●	1/2 mi.
9	DISHMILL CREEK	●	○	○	●	○	3 mi. *
10	BIG BEND	●	●	●	●	●	2 1/2 mi.
10A	TRILLIUM	●	○	○	●	○	1/2 mi.
11	DEER RUN	●	●	○	●	●	1 1/2 mi.
12	SENECA	●	○	○	●	○	3/4 mi.
13	ST. HELENA	●	○	○	●	○	1 1/4 mi.
14	GARDEAU	●	○	○	●	○	1/2 mi.
22	SYCAMORE	●	○	○	●	○	3/4 mi.
FLT	FINGER LAKES	●	★	○	●	○	24 mi.

This map shows Letchworth State Park as it is today. (Jeffrey Brooks, Letchworth State Park.)

LETCHWORTH STATE PARK

"The Grand Canyon of the East"

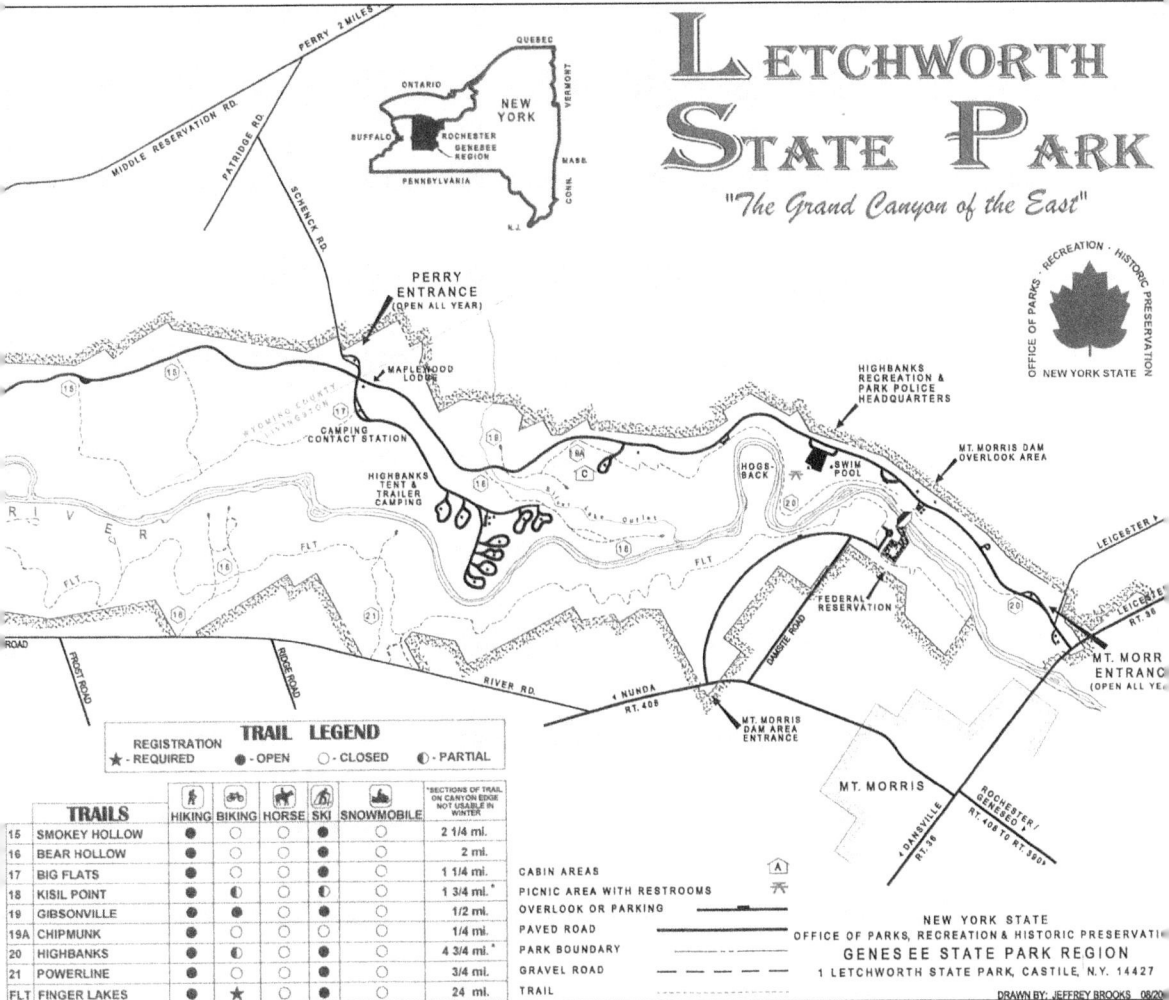

OFFICE OF PARKS · RECREATION · HISTORIC PRESERVATION
NEW YORK STATE

PERRY ENTRANCE (OPEN ALL YEAR)

MAPLEWOOD LODGE

HIGHBANKS RECREATION & PARK POLICE HEADQUARTERS

CAMPING CONTACT STATION

HIGHBANKS TENT & TRAILER CAMPING

MT. MORRIS DAM OVERLOOK AREA

HOGS-BACK

SWIM POOL

FEDERAL RESERVATION

MT. MORRIS ENTRANCE (OPEN ALL YEAR)

MT. MORRIS DAM AREA ENTRANCE

MT. MORRIS

NUNDA RT. 408

RIVER RD.

DANSVILLE RT. 36

ROCHESTER/GENESEO RT. 408 TO RT. 390

LEICESTER RT. 36

MIDDLE RESERVATION RD.

PATRIDGE RD.

SCHENCK RD.

FROST ROAD

RIDGE ROAD

RIVER

REGISTRATION — TRAIL LEGEND

★ - REQUIRED ● - OPEN ○ - CLOSED ◐ - PARTIAL

	TRAILS	HIKING	BIKING	HORSE	SKI	SNOWMOBILE	*SECTIONS OF TRAIL ON CANYON EDGE NOT USABLE IN WINTER
15	SMOKEY HOLLOW	●	○	○	●	○	2 1/4 mi.
16	BEAR HOLLOW	●	○	○	●	○	2 mi.
17	BIG FLATS	●	○	○	●	○	1 1/4 mi.
18	KISIL POINT	●	◐	○	◐	○	1 3/4 mi.*
19	GIBSONVILLE	●	●	○	●	○	1/2 mi.
19A	CHIPMUNK	●	○	○	○	○	1/4 mi.
20	HIGHBANKS	●	◐	○	●	○	4 3/4 mi.*
21	POWERLINE	●	○	○	●	○	3/4 mi.
FLT	FINGER LAKES	●	★	○	●	○	24 mi.

CABIN AREAS

PICNIC AREA WITH RESTROOMS

OVERLOOK OR PARKING

PAVED ROAD

PARK BOUNDARY

GRAVEL ROAD

TRAIL

NEW YORK STATE
OFFICE OF PARKS, RECREATION & HISTORIC PRESERVATION
GENESEE STATE PARK REGION
1 LETCHWORTH STATE PARK, CASTILE, N.Y. 14427

DRAWN BY: JEFFREY BROOKS 08/20

This tribute to the park's benefactor, written in 1909 by Sarah Evans Letchworth, appears on the memorial boulder at Inspiration Point: "God wrought for us this scene beyond compare, / But one man's loving hand protected it / And gave it to his fellow-men to share." (Letchworth State Park.)

BIBLIOGRAPHY

American Scenic and Historic Preservation Society. *Voices of the Glen*. New York: Knickerbocker Press, 1911.

Anderson, Mildred Lee Hills. *Genesee Echoes: The Upper Gorge and Falls Area from the Days of the Pioneers*. Dansville, NY: F. A. Owen Publishing Company, 1956.

———. *Gibsonville—the Vanished Village*. Dalton, NY: Burt's Printing Service, 1976.

———. *The Genesee Valley Canal, 1836–1878*. Self-published.

Anderson, Mildred Lee Hills, and Marian Piper Willey. *St. Helena—Ghost Town of the Genesee, 1797–1954*. Dalton, NY: Burt's Printing Service, 1970.

Barnes, Katherine. *Rainbow's End—The Story of Letchworth Park*. Perry, NY: Moxon Printing, 1967.

Beale, Irene A. *William P. Letchworth: A Man For Others*. Geneseo, NY: Chestnut Hill Press, 1982.

Bryant, William Cullen, ed. *Picturesque America*. Vol. II. New York: D. Appleton and Company, 1874.

Howland, Henry R. *The Caneadea Council House and Its Last Council Fire*. Perry, NY: Perry Herald, reprinted 1953.

Holton, Gladys Reid. *The Genesee Valley Canal*. Brockport, NY: Stylus Graphics, 1970.

Judkins, Russell A., ed. *League of the Iroquois: The Ethnographic Core of Lewis Henry Morgan's Classic Account of the Iroquois Confederacy*. North Andover, MA: Persimmon Press, 2004.

Larned, J. N. *The Life and Work of William Pryor Letchworth*. New York: Houghton Mifflin, 1912.

Letchworth Park Archives, Letchworth State Park, Castile, NY.

www.letchworthparkhistory.com

Parker, Arthur C. *Skunny Wundy and Other Indian Tales*. New York: George H. Doran Company, 1926.

Visit us at
arcadiapublishing.com

www.ingramcontent.com/pod-product-compliance
Lightning Source LLC
Chambersburg PA
CBHW050647110426
42813CB00007B/1942